Flipping the Switch

Flipping the Switch

FOUR PRINCIPLES OF SIGNIFICANT THINKING

Dr. Wm. Wayne Brown

Foreword by Andrew C. Yang, PGA

Copyright © 2015 Dr. Wm. Wayne Brown
All rights reserved.

ISBN: 1511694335
ISBN 13: 9781511694339
Library of Congress Control Number: 2015912693
CreateSpace Independent Publishing Platform
North Charleston, South Carolina

Acknowledgements

Throughout the process of writing this book, I have gained much encouragement from many sources. My family, friends, and colleagues have encouraged my efforts to the end result of publishing this work. My heartfelt gratitude goes out to each of you.

Special appreciation is due my First Read Review Team. Alphabetically, they are Todd Brown, Wendy Brown, Yvonne Brown, Helen Elsasser, Judy Flora, Angela Johnson, David Johnson, Sean Ludeman, and Gwen Rapp. You have done a masterful job of pointing out blindsides and deficits, as well as the quality of the manuscript.

It is a profound honor to be allowed into the lives of the interviewees whose stories are shared in these pages. You have enriched both my life and my writing. Your willingness to share deeply personal struggles and successes required trust on your part. Thank you for your participation and encouragement. I am confident the readers will gain much inspiration from your stories.

Thank you to Andrew Yang for not only participating in the interview process, but also for writing the foreword to *Flipping the Switch*.

Wm. Wayne Brown, Ed.D.

To my wife, Yvonne:

For her encouragement and inspiration
each time I needed to flip the switch
and get back on task.

Contents

Acknowledgements · v

Foreword ·xi

Introduction ·xiii

Chapter 1 The Beginning of a Journey · · · · · · · · · · · · · · · · · 1

Chapter 2 Who Are You, Really? · 9

Chapter 3 Significant Thinking Principle #1 · · · · · · · · · · · 16

Chapter 4 Significant Thinking Principle #2 · · · · · · · · · · · 25

Chapter 5 Significant Thinking Principle #3 · · · · · · · · · · · 34

Chapter 6 Significant Thinking Principle #4 · · · · · · · · · · · 47

Chapter 7	Facing Your Fears and Worries · · · · · · · · · · · · · 58
Chapter 8	Consolidate Your Power, Not Your Problems · 71
Chapter 9	Four Aspects of Problems · · · · · · · · · · · · · · · · · · · 81
Chapter 10	Personal Perspective and Attitude · · · · · · · · · 95
Chapter 11	If You're Not Yet a Diamond, At Least Be Semiprecious · · · · · · · · · · · · · · · · · · 115
Chapter 12	Tripping Points & Tipping Points · · · · · · · · · · 127
Chapter 13	Step into Your Future · 147
	About Dr. Wm. Wayne Brown · · · · · · · · · · · · 163

Foreword

I first met Dr. Wayne Brown when he came to me for instruction about his golf swing. Though that's where the relationship began, it soon blossomed and included many topics of conversation about life. I remember Wayne's deep enthusiasm to improve his swing, but his positive attitude and strength of mind were the driving forces behind real improvement. I was excited to have him as a student as he knew the kind of work it took to get better. As our relationship grew, I discovered he was writing a book, and I could not wait to read it, let alone be featured as one of his stories.

Through this exciting book, Wayne Brown gives us great insight into how we think and interact with ourselves and other people. His stories shed light on the origins of some of our deepest problems that in turn can help us decide how to "flip the switch." He shows us his coaching applications are extremely useful in our daily thoughts and gives us a new way to get the ball rolling.

As a golf coach, I must realize that every individual is different and must be coached differently, but the ones who discover the most success are the ones who have mentally decided that they "can." Wayne teaches us how we can mentally decide that we "can" in order to achieve our goals, whatever they may be. Even though this is not a book about golf instruction, there is so much that we can reap from Wayne to improve our personal situations. The game of golf is similar to the game of life—we need to "flip the switch" in order to achieve desired results. I cannot wait to begin implementing Wayne's practices into my teaching.

Enjoy "flipping your switch."

Andrew C. Yang, PGA Director of Golf
The Futures Course at the 500 Club
Scottsdale, Arizona

Introduction

Overall, this is a book of encouragement and empowerment toward a more fulfilled lifestyle. It is generated from my own life, studies, learnings, interviews, research, observations, and experiences. I begin by saying what this book is not. It is *not*

- primarily academic, though it is backed by scholarship;
- overtly religious, though it is spiritual; or
- just another positive-thinking book, though the contents are full of hope and help to aid you on your journey toward a more positive lifestyle.

This book *is*

- a voice saying that you can have a more fulfilling lifestyle by changing the process of your thinking and then taking action on that thinking;

- a resource toward a more fulfilling lifestyle;
- a new way of processing how you think about yourself and your life;
- a practical guide to the autonomy of your own mentality;
- a pathway toward allowing your spirit to soar;
- encouragement to write your history by creating your future; and
- a reflective rather than a reactive process.

I encourage you to think, not plow. In other words, instead of charging through these brief pages, it is my hope that you will stop and reflect as you read. The contents of this book are intended for you and your reflections. If they seem to apply to someone else, share them with that person. Still, it really is about you at this point. Read, stop, and reflect. Read some more, stop, and reflect. I will try to remind you to do that from time to time. If you are a self-directed thinker, you may need no reminder at all.

I titled the book *Flipping the Switch* because fulfillment should not be postponed—or, even worse, abandoned altogether. There is no do-over for any day we have. Each has its rewards, even in the face of challenges, but only when you make the decision to move forward. "Flipping the switch" from inertia to movement is a tremendously rewarding and challenging process. Just knowing you are working on it and taking action will help bring you a sense of peace, joy, and accomplishment.

In this book, you will examine four significant thinking principles that will guide and help you change your thinking and begin to move toward a more rewarding life. These significant thinking principles will serve as a mirror for your thinking and reflect the significance of the *way* you think. It is my belief and experience that changing the way an individual thinks greatly affects the outcome of his or her thinking. I will use the personal pronoun *you* a great deal here. Because after all, this really is about you. While it is true that the world does not revolve around you, your world *does* revolve around you. Make it stellar!

As a bonus, if you complete this book and put into practice these efforts toward flipping the switch in your life, I will do my best to share some of your journey. Probably the best way to do that is through a blog, the content of which will come from readers' questions, comments, and insights. I am not a licensed counselor or therapist, but my education, personal experiences, and work with adults qualify me to share these resources with you as you move toward achievement, fulfillment, and enrichment.

CHAPTER 1

The Beginning of a Journey

It was darker than the inside of a black cat at midnight. My mood exactly matched my environment, which was cold. Very cold. Snow blanketed the concrete sidewalk on which my steps fell with a crunchiness that only exaggerated my sense of being alone. It was late fall in Arlington, Virginia, but it was deep winter in my soul.

More than a year earlier, my mother and two high school friends had driven me to college to begin my academic career. During that first semester, I struggled with lots of issues. One was my naïveté about what college was like. I had been totally unprepared for the shock of the cultural change. Having come from a small high school in an agriculturally based, county seat town, I had been prepared for college in the humanities much more than in the realities of life. In this case, the reality of being expelled from college.

I was so green that a new shade of the color should have been created by Sherwin-Williams, named after me, and sold with my picture on the bucket. There was no one to give me guidance, counsel, or advice in my new surroundings, even to help me make good course selections. Despite having had chemistry and physics in high school, I failed my first semester six-hour course and lab in chemistry. I had been so hopelessly lost that the professor had insisted that I need not take the final!

That had been devastating enough, but my situation worsened. My music professor had also seen the train wreck coming. His first clue was when I mispronounced "Beethoven" during class! When asked to identify any of the musical movements, it became too much like intestinal distress for me. Music appreciation class made me lose my appreciation for classical music, not to be regained until many years later. Two more semester hours failed. Sherwin-Williams green!

It wasn't that I didn't study. I studied very hard. But I still had failing grades in more than half of my first semester courses. Although I redoubled my efforts, I was drowning in worry, and eventually, I became ill due to eating little and resting even less. Mercifully, that semester finally ground to an end.

My second semester seemed more hopeful. I became a solid and confident C student—a huge improvement from the first semester. I realized that I never should have begun my college years with the sciences, even though my counselor had advised it. Unbeknownst to me, fate was about to intervene. Toward the end of the second semester, the dean of students summoned me to his office for a little chat.

I hate it when people say, "I have something I need to *chat* with you about." Such statements usually wind up devoid of good things. Our little "chat" had gone something like this:

"Mr. Brown, you have failed to maintain a passing grade during your freshman year. Therefore, you are being expelled from the college."

"Yes, sir, I know my first semester was a disaster. But my second semester was much improved. I should never have started with the sciences. I know how to better choose my courses now. May I please stay, based on my second semester improvement?" I pleaded.

"No," he replied blankly. He had a stuffy, humorless personality that revealed no love for higher education. I wondered what I had done to tick this guy off so much! There was no acknowledgment of my second semester improvement, no words of encouragement whatsoever.

"What can I do to change your mind?" I asked.

"Nothing."

"What if I stayed and went to summer school to pull up my GPA?"

"That won't help—we've already made our decision."

I strongly suspected that *we* was actually *he*.

"Then what should I do next?"

"You should leave." If that was a try at humor, it didn't work.

So that was it. I had been kicked out. The only people I'd known who had been kicked out of college were the ones who violated the drinking policy. I had never even had a beer in my life up to that point. My devotion to the rules had done nothing to soften the dean's decision.

Thus, having had my posterior handed to me, I left. I had been so numb and upset that I later could not recall leaving his office and walking back to my dormitory. I sat on the edge of my bed until dinnertime was announced by the usual chiming of the chapel bells. To me, they sounded more mocking than uplifting. I had been disgraced.

■ ■ ■

To say it impacted me to the point of serious depression and despair is an understatement. I did not have a single human soul with whom I could talk about my despair. I did pray a lot, but in a way, that almost seemed to make it worse. Let me explain. I was severely impacted by my failure for three important reasons.

First, although I loved to joke and have fun, inside I was always a terribly serious and dutiful person. During my senior year of high school, I'd been voted "Male Most Likely to Succeed." Martha Horning had been my female counterpart.

"I'll bet *she* didn't flunk out of college," I thought sadly.

In light of my failure and self-perceived uselessness, that silly title brought pain whenever I remembered it. I didn't really understand what true success was until many years later.

Second, but most importantly, I had failed two entities that were hugely important to me: my family and my church. I had been sent off to college with high expectations, pride, and many prayers for my success. My mother had worked two jobs to help me afford college tuition. I had now let *everyone* down, including myself.

The last reason, and perhaps most frightening, concerned my relationship with God. Feeling there was a spiritual purpose and destiny for my life, I had even let God down! I had gone to college to prepare myself for where God was leading me. But instead of becoming prepared, I had now become even more unprepared. I had *lost* ground, for crying out loud! Stripped of my sense of purpose and identity, I began to think maybe I had been wrong about it from the beginning.

I felt there was no one to talk to about it. At least, no one who could help. Nor did the dean suggest anyone to me. Certainly, there was no one who could fix it but *me*. I was more correct than I knew. However, during the second semester, one person had given me encouragement. That had been Professor Lane Wells. I really only fully appreciated his encouragement years later as I reflected on those difficult times. Finally, after so many years, I contacted him last year to thank him for his encouragement.

So I kept it inside. Rationalizing that many students failed only made me feel worse. I didn't *want* to be included in that club. Compounding my depression were my worries about finances, telling my family I had flunked out, and my recent breakup with my girlfriend. No amount of rationalization or justification about others failing college was going to help. This was about me, not somebody else. I felt like a loser. I *was* a loser.

With no job and no money, one of my sisters mercifully invited me to live with her in Arlington, Virginia. I found employment with the Veterans Administration Central Office in Washington, DC. It was a boring, mind-numbing clerical job crunching numbers all day, but I was very thankful to have it. And it had a great title: Assistant to the Director of White House Data Processing. Basically, I was part of a summer government intern program begun by President John F. Kennedy.

At the end of each day, I rode a bus out of the district back to Arlington where I was a Safeway cashier each evening until closing. On Saturdays, I usually worked at the store all day.

So it was, on that cold, dark night in Arlington, Virginia. I had just finished a long day of work at the Veterans Administration and Safeway. As I walked back to my sister's apartment, I had plenty of time to think about what had happened in my life over the past year and a half since leaving college, how tired I was, and how disillusioned I had become. And all that before the age of twenty. At least I was excelling in something!

On that lonely night's walk, something profound happened in my life. I became angry. Really angry. Deeply angry. I had never been one to express my feelings very much. I had not yet learned that the saying, "Men don't cry," was comparable to what came out the south end of a northbound horse. I didn't cry that night either. Rather, it was something that welled up inside me, and somehow, someway, it flipped a switch inside my mind and soul.

I flipped that switch mentally out of anger at myself. I wasn't angry at the college or at my lack of money. I wasn't even angry at the situation. I became angry that something which I felt was deeply important had been snatched away from me. I had lost my dignity and self-respect. Sometimes the best-placed anger is that which we aim at ourselves. That is, if it's used for motivation and not for self-condemnation.

I also became very afraid. And this is crucial...I was afraid that *the state of being in which I had found myself was all there was going to be for me.* I would have to settle for my life situation as it was presented to me at that very moment. Was there anything wrong with being a government worker and making a career out of that? Nothing at all. Government service is an admirable occupation, but it wasn't what I wanted. Was there anything wrong with working at a grocery store and making that part of my life? Again, nothing wrong with it at all. Not everyone needs to go to college or even should, but for me, it was a foundational part of getting ready for the rest of my life. It wasn't as much about the college degree as it was about my own personal failure.

Anger and fear were the two catalysts that flipped the switch for me. Something turned over inside my mind and soul, and I determined at that moment that I would return to the same college and I *would* graduate. It became such an instant and compelling force within me that my resolve became a living thing, indescribably galvanized. I expressed my sense of clarity: "I will not let this defeat me, and I will do something with my life, so help me God!"

I reapplied to the same college and was admitted with a one-semester probationary period attached. I returned to college somewhat emotionally bruised but wiser. Significantly, I learned to make the system work for me. I worked hard, embraced the academic experience, and graduated from a school that I grew to love. The shadow of my earlier failure was a constant catalyst pushing me forward, and I eventually stopped looking over my shoulder and began looking ahead. After graduating from college, I married my soul mate, earned my master's degree, and later earned a doctorate in education and business from a Big Ten university. Later, I was privileged to teach graduate school for a while and loved the academic aspects of my life. The switch had flipped, and my personal history had been avenged. Importantly, not all the lessons I learned were academic.

CHAPTER 2

Who Are You, Really?

Look, your story is not mine, and mine is not yours. But there are principles at work that can help you flip the switch that is inside you. Flipping the switch is not just moving *from* something—it is moving *toward* something. In moving toward something, what you gain is almost always so much more than what you give up. One of the saddest things I witness in life is observing people who want to do something with their lives but never actually take steps to do it. Equally sad is moving through life with seemingly no understanding of what a blessing it is to *have* it, and no desire to give anything back.

Why is that? You're not lazy, or you wouldn't be reading this book. No, it's more than that. One of the big reasons for lack of personal fulfillment is *inertia*. Physics teaches us that a body at rest resists movement. Once movement begins, it is much easier to keep the momentum going. I encourage you to walk with me through this book on your way to building momentum toward a more rewarding and fulfilling personal life.

It is important for you to understand that personal fulfillment is not necessarily going from one career choice to another. Nor is it about how much money you can earn. For example, if you are a bricklayer, it doesn't mean you have to become an astronaut. Bricklaying is an honorable and ancient trade. What is important is fulfillment, *not position*. They are not the same thing.

Understand that fulfillment in your life may or may not be brought about by your position or your career. Indeed, your path toward a sense of enrichment may lead from the White House to the log cabin, instead of the other way around. Flipping your own switch is a determination only you can make in light of your values and your deep-seated longing for personal satisfaction. This book is designed to walk with you and aid you on your journey toward life decisions that will give rise to a greater sense of accomplishment.

You may be a very busy parent with a job, a house, a spouse, a pet, and sports schedules. And you may feel totally consumed by it all. If you are basically fulfilled and enriched even in the face of all the demands, then you probably don't want to change those parts of your life situation. In that case, you may feel a lack of fulfillment in other areas that are not being addressed, such as personal relationships, purposeful work, health, body image, intellectual stimulation, and more. The point is that *you* get to choose where you want to make progress toward greater life quality and meaningfulness. Only *you* can decide if you need professional help in some of those areas.

So who are you, really? I warn you not to answer that question too quickly. To do so may cause you to miss some truly significant insights. Who you are is not necessarily what you do for a living. Please read that sentence again. Many people think they know all about themselves when they may know only part of it. And you would be very wrong if you think older adults are the only ones set in their ways. All ages have blind sides concerning how they view themselves, their abilities, their likes and dislikes, how others perceive them, and how they perceive their own thinking patterns.

Consider that most of us know our personal histories much better than we know and understand the significance of the present. And we are often resistant to examining the future. Each day we live, we stand in the *middle* of our own personal history. We stand between the past and the future, and that point moves each day. So the future becomes the present every single day. How we interact with that reality on a daily basis can make a huge difference in changing our future history.

Getting beyond resistance to movement can be hard. Or perhaps you are trying to help someone else on his or her journey to flip the switch from inertia to movement. Colonel Sanders could never have created his Kentucky Fried Chicken empire without first actually trying to cook a chicken. Some of his recipes simply did not work out for him. He also had to know what he did well. Eventually, with great effort, he was able to turn failure into finger-licking-good success!

Throughout this book, you will be challenged to examine your reflective statements. A huge part of that examination is deciding *who* you want to be. It is an enormously important consideration because most people think in terms of *what* they want to be: a teacher, a fireman, a doctor, a minister, etc. Those considerations are important in flipping the switch, but at the base of it all is *who* you will become. Some frequent questions asked of young people include:

"*What* do you want to be when you grow up?"

"*What* do you want to be when you graduate?"

The Graduate is a classic example of our *who/what* orientation. At the graduation party for the character played by Dustin Hoffman, a well-meaning friend of the family says to him in a conspiratorial voice, "I have one word for you. Plastics!" Of course, we wouldn't have remembered a line in the movie that said, "I have one word of advice for you. Know *who* you want to be!"

Knowing who you are is just as important as knowing what you are. Maria Shriver's book *Just Who Will You Be?* makes some very good points in that regard. She writes the following:

> I now realize that everyone I've ever met in my life who's interesting, who has a life of deep meaning and joy, is still open to new answers to that question, new opportunities for change and growth.
>
> And it doesn't have to be a cataclysmic shift on the outside. It can be a seismic shift on the inside. Signing up for school on the Internet. Refocusing on your health and doing something real about it. Beginning and sticking with a spiritual practice.

Committing to sitting quietly with yourself twenty minutes a day to see what you learn. (Use commuting time for that!)

The change doesn't have to be huge, but it may have to be deep. A deep change for me was realizing I'd have to take the time to know what I *feel*, in order to know *who* I am and *who* I want to be.

I have developed the following parts of the self-examination and self-preparation process.

Take a helicopter ride. Imagine yourself in a helicopter looking down on your life's history. Where you have been in your life is a good clue to your present and future history. While where you have been is not to be relied on completely for shaping your future, it has been formative in getting you to this point of your life and cannot be ignored. Examine your job and career choices. Why did you accept the job you have now? Because it pays well? That's important, and it's not bad if it isn't the only fulfillment you get from your job.

Why did you choose to marry or remain single? If you are married, why did you marry that person? If you are single, is it by choice or because of pain? How much do those choices impact your life now? These are just examples. Many other questions can be raised as you take your helicopter ride.

Such questions may cause turbulence on your ride. If so, you will want to do some examination of where and why the turbulence is there. You may need to see a professional, perhaps one recommended by your physician. If you do see a therapist or other professional consultant, remember that your chemistry with that person is very important. Keep looking until you find someone with whom you can relate, but not necessarily with whom you feel totally comfortable. Comfort may not be what you need, but rather honesty, competency, and motivation.

How do you want your future to look? Where do you want to go? I find that many people don't really know what they want to do with their future. Perhaps you fall into that category. If so, this book will help you develop the resources to think through your present and future choices, thereby bringing more fulfillment, clarity, and meaning for you.

It may be that you *do* know where you want to go, but you just can't seem to flip the switch from inertia to forward movement. Whether you know or don't know, your future is happening right now. In either of these two cases, there are resources to help place your hand on the switch, overcome inertia, and move forward. The rest of this book is a resource to aid you in that process.

For you to flip your switch from neutral to drive, you will need to get a good case of motivation. No one can do that for you. You must determine that you will do something about those areas of your life that make you unhappy, bored, unfulfilled, or just uncertain. Also know that it will not be easy. If you have ever pushed a stalled car from a dead stop, you know how hard it is to get it moving. But once it's moving, it's easier to keep it moving.

Making It Personal
It is essential that you to take inventory of yourself up to this point. Begin your journey toward flipping the switch by grabbing a pencil, asking yourself these questions, and writing your answers down. Become a "Where Wolf."

1. **Where have I been in my life to this point?** Identify the watershed moments in your past, giving each one the respect it deserves. Try to assess the impact each one has made on your life. *Stalk those watershed moments*. For example, the epiphany moment on that cold night in Arlington was a watershed moment for me.
2. **Where am I now?** Determine your "Sitz im Leben"—your real situation in life. Identify your reality at this point. Is it what you thought it would be? How satisfied are you with it? *Thoughtfully stalk those reflections*.
3. **In what direction do I want my life to travel?** Where do I want my life to go? Even if you are totally content with your life at this point, the future will come. Dream about that future a little. *Stalk your potential.*
4. **Through it all, *who* have I become?** Am I a self-directed person on the path of a life that has purpose and meaning?

CHAPTER 3

Significant Thinking Principle #1

*Any thinking that does not move
you forward diminishes you.*
(SIGNIF-**I-CAN'T**)

If you can honestly say to yourself that your life circumstances are exactly on track and where you want them, then you can close this book. You flipped your switch long ago. Congratulations!

However, if your life is not going where you want it to go, then read on. It is my firm belief that achievement and fulfillment come from one's heart and mind. The Psalmist wrote, "As a person thinks in their heart, so are they." No one gets to decide for you if your dreams and goals are appropriate and realistic. That's not fair. They don't get to choose for you. Nevertheless, to move forward, you will need to do what I call "significant thinking." There are some significant thinking principles (STPs) associated with moving forward. The principles lie in the word "significant" itself. They are simple but not simplistic, revealing but not obvious.

Part of flipping the switch in anyone's heart and mind is saying and believing, "This (situation, failure, unfulfilled existence, stalemate, etc.) is beneath me! I will not tolerate staying in this life situation." This is also called self-respect. One of the reasons I feel compelled to write this book is because for years I have seen people who needed to flip the switch, but received little or no encouragement or challenge to do so. It has been my privilege to extend a hand to some of those people to help put their hands on the switch.

To work toward flipping the switch is far preferable to living the *Prometheus Bound* existence. You will recall that in Greek mythology, Prometheus really ticked off Zeus when he gave the gift of fire to humanity. Zeus not only punished Prometheus but had his best friend, Hephaestus, carry out the sentence! Prometheus was bound to a huge rock upon which his liver was eaten daily by birds, only to have it heal again through the night, and then eaten out again the next day, over and over.

Similarly, Sisyphus was compelled to roll an enormous boulder up a hill, only to watch it roll back down every time. Push it up the hill, watch it roll back down, over and over and over.

Without taking steps to move from inertia to personal advancement toward fulfillment, you are doomed to live the kind of existence in which your life is sucked out daily.

I have watched people who were trying to move forward but needed some wise, compassionate, yet objective guidance. Some of those people were low on self-awareness. Tom was one of those people. He had interviewed for several positions and could never quite pull the trigger on getting hired. After being turned down for a second position for which he was very well qualified, it occurred to me that maybe Tom's problem was not his qualifications but his performance during the interviews. I suspected that Tom lacked self-awareness about how he was being perceived.

I had Tom tell me some of the questions he was asked, and then I asked him those same questions and added some of my own. I was shocked when this man, who was rather reserved, came across like the verbal hounds of hell! He couldn't stop talking. He gave answers to the questions and even gave answers to questions that hadn't been asked! He continued until the shades were coming down on any interest I had in his answers. Even his body language came across as aggressive and arrogant. He had absolutely no realization of how he was being perceived. There was no self-awareness.

Tom and I had a disagreement and then an agreement. When people ask for help, they don't always like what they hear. Finally, it was agreed that we would work on his body language and voice modulation so that he presented a demeanor of sincerity, pleasantness, and openness without appearing too eager and aggressive. That approach was not deceptive, because he really was a sincere person. It just wasn't manifesting itself.

Through video playback, we spent significant time working on his answers, keeping them short, to the point, and pleasant. Then we would find a good stopping point and actually stop! We repeated our role-playing, and with coaching, he did much better. Eventually, Tom secured another job interview. The potential employer was someone with whom I had the kind of relationship that allowed Tom to ask for a very unusual favor.

His potential employer was asked for permission for me, his coach, to be a passive observer in the interview. And they allowed it! In fact, it was seen as a positive for several reasons. It said to the potential employer that he was interviewing someone who could think outside the box. It told him that Tom was someone who truly wanted to do his best and was willing to be observed by his coach in a live interview. It gave the employer a chance to see what coaching results might do for other staff already on the payroll. And Tom's willingness to be vulnerable in a stressful situation spoke volumes about his maturity.

Two weeks later Tom called with the happy news that he had secured the job. For him, the whole process took him from how he *thought* he was being perceived to a new awareness of how he was *really* coming across. He went from "*I can't* get a job" to "If I can change how I present myself, then *I can* get the job I want."

■ ■ ■

A word about life coaches or mentors. Yes, a truly gifted life coach or mentor can help guide you. The coach should not be afraid of hurting his or her protégé's feelings. However, once a path is being opened up in significant thinking, and an individual begins to sense that there is a direction, the coach must encourage, prod, challenge, reflect, and sometimes become directive. But the real responsibility is with you. Here's how it works.

Embedded in the word "significant" are the words "I can't." The "I can't" statements in our lives can be reactive or reflective. Reactive statements are the ones that come out of real or perceived (perception is reality at some level) actions taken for or against you by *others*. Similarly, reflective statements are the ones that come out of real or perceived actions we take for or against *ourselves*.

> I React ← Reactive Statements
> Reflective Statements → I Think
> Also
> Past Oriented ← Reactive Statements
> Reflective Statements → Future Oriented

A reactive statement might sound something like

- "I was hurt so badly by that person that *I can't* get over it";
- "They did me so dirty at that company that *I can't* shake my negative attitude toward them";
- "My spouse had an affair and *I can't* get over it";
- "I lost my job and, with it, the sense of security I once had. *I can't* deal with that."

Think of your own past experiences and recall those times when you may have had life situations that evoked reactive statements that included "I can't." Is it possible that, for you, these events live on within your reactive thinking?

Reactive statements may also come out of those times when we have bruised our own lives. I call these autoreactive statements. For example, an autoreactive statement may sound like

- "I regret how I treated my child/parent/spouse/friend so much that *I can't* open up enough to ask for forgiveness and reestablish some kind of relationship";
- "I regret that I never finished high school/went to college/took that job I was offered. *I can't* forgive myself for missing the boat";
- "I messed up my life, then gave my child up for adoption. *I can't* get over the sense of guilt."

There is an almost limitless supply of examples. Think about those times in your life when you were in situations that, because of your own actions, were causing you to give yourself autoreactive "I can't" statements here in the present. This is one of those times where I am prompting you to actually stop and reflect. Please do yourself a favor and jot down the thoughts that come to your mind about this section. It could be important in unlocking and getting rid of some unwanted baggage that is holding you back emotionally, physically, or spiritually. Try using this autoreactive statement to help get you started: "I can't get past what I did when I _____." Please do it now.

Reflective statements are very different. These are statements that emerge from your thinking process, but also ones that make you *think* about them instead of shutting down. By contrast, statements that are reactive to what happened in the past just sit inside your mind and ulcerate your perspective. Or they may take you to the cross streets of Depression Avenue and Anger Boulevard. "I can't" simply shuts the door.

Using the above seven examples, let's rephrase one into a reflective statement. "They did me so dirty at that company that I can't shake my negative attitude toward them." Rephrased as a reflective statement, it may look like this: "They did me so dirty at that company (you aren't denying your feelings) that I have had a hard time getting over it. But as I think clearly about it, I learned a lot about myself, the corporate world, and *now* I can use those things to make me stronger in my career."

Reflective statements don't deny the pain and the reality. Not at all! Instead, they acknowledge it and look for something that can be salvaged from the situation as a takeaway benefit, enabling forward movement. Reflective statements *empower*, whereas reactive statements go nowhere and *diminish*. Remember, *thinking that does not move you forward diminishes you*.

Reflect on whether your current situation is indicative of situations in life that bring about reactive "I can't" statements. Can you bring yourself to change those reactive statements into reflective statements? The latter can help you move toward flipping the switch in a direction that is more positive and productive for your fulfillment and your future.

It can be difficult to keep reactive statements from renting space in your head. To an extent, the admonition "Keep your enemies close" is true. Keep your enemy statements close to you for only as long as it takes to identify them and decide whether they are reactive ones (you've been acted upon, and you are reacting negatively) or if they are reflective ones (you or someone else has done the action, and you are thinking your way through it).

Imagine that you are the quarterback of a football team. All during the game, the opposing team has scored on you, badly bashing your team's defenses. It's been a long afternoon. And now, you have the ball on your own five-yard line, and it's fourth down. Only two minutes remain on the clock. It doesn't look good for your team. Do you just walk off the field and forfeit the game? Of course not! "They've scored on us all afternoon and things look bleak. I can't do anything about this situation." That would be a reactive statement.

A reflective statement would be "I know what has happened in this game, and I know it looks bad, but I have the ball!" The significant thinking here is *I have the ball*. That realization gives options, not just in a football game but also in life situations. Regardless of what has happened in the past, the thing to remember is that you have the ball. To just give up would be doing a great injustice to yourself, and perhaps to those around you.

In the end, you have to decide how much of yourself you are willing to sell in order to stay in the "I can't" thinking mode. And you *will* sell something. It might be physical health, mental health, a relationship, or some other trade-off. And who is the buyer to whom you sell those pieces of yourself? "I can't" is the buyer! And it has no right to own any part of you.

CHAPTER 4

Significant Thinking Principle #2

As thinking begins to open up, so do possibilities.
(SIGN-**IF-I-CAN'T**)

Significant thinking is more than merely telling yourself to think positively. It's a matter of *how* you think. It's about training your mind to think in a powerfully new way about yourself and your surroundings. Opening your mind to thinking that is both significant and worthy of you is like letting a fresh breeze blow across your heart and soul.

Also embedded in the word "significant" are the words "if I can't." There is a difference between saying "I can't" and saying "*if* I can't." When someone says "I can't," he has dug his heels into the ground of inertia, firmly claiming that landscape as his own. Yet when someone says "if I can't," it indicates he has not fully ruled out the possibility of flipping the switch.

"If I can't" thinking causes the thinker to raise his or her eyes ever so slightly from the ground to the *implications of not taking action*. Those implications are hugely important. They are implications that must be examined. Declaring "if I can't" brings into somewhat clearer focus the implications of what lies ahead as a result of not dealing with the issue. That is, it allows contingencies to exist that may become unpleasant.

Some of those "if I can't" statements may be analogous to the following:

- "*If I can't* bring myself to do something about my sense of being stuck, then I will have to be in this agony for a long time." This is a reactive statement with some openness.
- "*If I can't* bring about change in my lack of feeling fulfilled, then it will affect others around me." This is a reactive statement with some openness beyond oneself to others.
- "*If I can't* seriously examine the potential of my life, then at least a part of my life is going to be unfulfilled, if not wasted." This is a reactive statement, but moving in the right direction.

This part of significant thinking points to more than feeling nailed to the floor by inertia. Eventually, the individual must decide whether to open his mind to the possibility of flipping the switch in a direction that is different from his current discomfort. Singer-songwriter Alicia Keyes expresses it well: "And the day came when the risk it took to remain tight and closed in the bud was more painful than the risk it took to bloom. This is the element of freedom."

Georgiana is a woman for whom I served as life coach and mentor, and who came to my office on a regular basis. At the time of my association with her, she was a single woman in her early to midthirties. Georgiana lived with her parents. She had always lived with her parents, even when she attended college. She still lived with her parents, even though she had a full-time job with a software company. The sticking point with Georgiana was that she did not *want* to keep living with her parents.

"Do you find it fulfilling to live with your parents?" I asked her once.

"I love my parents, but I don't find living with them fulfilling," she replied.

"What is the discomfort about living there?"

"Well, they tell me what to do all the time," she said. "I don't feel like I'm living my own life."

"You must like it that way," I offered.

She shot back. "No, I don't like it that way!"

"Why don't you like it that way?"

"Because I'm grown and I can make my own decisions. I can make up my own mind about what I should and should not do!"

"Okay," I continued. "Is either parent in need, such that you feel compelled to live there and help out?"

"Oh, no, they're very healthy, and both have good incomes."

"Then you must have made up your own mind that you will remain living with your parents and put up with the dissatisfaction, because that's where you are," I contended.

"They get involved in all my decisions, especially my mother," she said.

"You must like it that way," I replied.

"No, I'm telling you, I *don't* like it that way!" she answered, but with less conviction than her earlier reply.

"What gets under your skin about all this?"

"I like to make my own decisions and know that I'm capable of taking care of myself."

I repeated, "Then you must have made up your mind that you will remain living with your parents and deal with the discomfort, because that's where you are."

Exchanges like these were usually accompanied by a lot of tears and emotion—on her part, not mine! Georgiana came back for many sessions. Each session I tried to probe her mind about why she continued to live in a way that was unsatisfactory to her. Why *wouldn't* she get her own apartment? Why *wouldn't* she enjoy a fulfilling life that included her parents, but was separate from them in day-to-day living and decision-making?

During the third or fourth session, the switch finally flipped. We began as usual with complaints about her parents continuing to control her life and how unhappy she was. She complained that she was never going to meet any guys and how no one ever asked her out. Once again, I pointed out the obvious.

"Georgiana, you simply have to get your own place. You can afford it."

"But I can't do that to my parents! They enjoy me living there, and I'm the only child."

"Have you ever considered that you express a lot of 'I can't' statements? You say you can't get your own apartment. You can't make your own decisions. You can't keep a good relationship with your mother if you move out. You can't find someone to date. You can't ever get married and have a family. I would like for you to try something. In the next few days, be conscious of and count how many times you use or think the words 'I can't.' I believe you'll be surprised, if not alarmed, at how many limitations you put on yourself."

The next time we met, Georgiana told me she'd tried to count her "I can't" statements. She admitted that they were numerous. She confessed that she'd even said she couldn't go out to dinner with some colleagues because her parents were preparing dinner at home.

"Georgiana, I think you use 'I can't' statements to avoid getting started with moving forward with your life. Most of your 'I can't' statements are self-imposed or autoreactive. I think you're more frightened of your future than leaving your inertia."

"But that's not true."

"Tell me why it's not true," I invited.

Georgiana couldn't think of any reasons why my statement wasn't true. Tears ensued.

Gently but firmly, I said, "Georgiana, you are not making progress in resolving your angst. Here's the telephone. If you don't pick it up and call this personal friend of mine who is an apartment manager to see an apartment, then I don't think I can meet with you again."

Somewhat shocked and with trembling hands and tearful eyes, she dialed the number. Georgiana did flip the switch and decided that she would get her own place. She eventually demonstrated this by her posture, her demeanor, her clothes, and, most thrillingly, by her smile. She later met and married a fine young man with whom she eventually had children. Georgiana canned the self-imposed "I can't" statements and began to bloom!

The pain of staying in her inertia had become her closest friend. But that friend began to melt away as her desire for a more meaningful life made the pain of doing nothing more painful than doing something.

Many of Georgiana's statements in our conversations were reactive statements. She responded out of a sense of what was being done to her.

"My parents don't want me to move out."

"My mom will be upset with me."

"Dad and mom will think I don't love them."

"My parents supplement my income by providing my housing and food."

The statements reflected what she perceived was being imposed upon her, rather than giving her ways to be reflective upon the possibilities. She had even stated, "I'm comfortable this way."

It was interesting to note that after she had become more self-directed in her life, her parents were very happy for her. Her parents were not what was holding her back. It was Georgiana's own reactive thinking that imposed restrictions upon her.

■ ■ ■

Interestingly, the *Encarta World English Dictionary* gives two definitions of the word *if*:

- A conjunction used to indicate the circumstances that would have to exist in order for an event to happen. (That one isn't too bad.)
- A conjunction used to indicate a modification to a statement, usually to add something negative or to indicate that there is less of something than originally expected. (Better but still not on target. Just too negative!)

Those are good definitions that underscore conditions, and they underscore the importance of guiding one's own thinking in ways that are significant and personal. I'm no dictionary, yet I see a huge component to *if* that is being missed. *Encarta* misses the major component of *if* as an introduction to the possibility of *positive* outcomes. For example, suppose someone says, "*If* I can get help with my situation, then my life and those of my family will be more secure." That's very different from "I can't get help with my situation." I'm sure you can see the subtle but very significant and real impact that words have on our thinking.

Realization of this principle—that as thinking begins to open up, so do possibilities—was a part of my own personal switch that was flipped on that cold winter's night in Virginia. That realization has required reaffirmation at various intervals in my life. It will for you, as well.

Making It Personal

Please pause and reflect on this question: What "if I can't" statements move you emotionally? Now, connect those statements to positive outcomes.

For example, "*If I can't* change my mental and physical condition, then my family may suffer. Therefore, I *must* flip the switch toward a better mental and physical self so that not only I but also my family will have a better quality of life."

Finally, write out a plan for achieving those positive outcomes. I know it sounds simple, but externalizing your steps forward is very important.

CHAPTER 5
Significant Thinking Principle #3

Moonlight is better than no light.
(SIGN-**IF-I-CAN**-T)

Light begins to dawn even when there is only a moon. Significant thinking moves from "I can't" through "if I can't" to the still somewhat tenuous but more productive thinking represented by "if I can."

From northwestern Canada, there is a watershed called the Continental Divide that stretches south including the Rocky Mountains and continuing down into New Mexico. It is a line that divides the runoff flow of water between the Pacific Ocean and the Atlantic Ocean.

Precipitation in the form of rain or snow that drains on the west side of the divide flows toward the Pacific Ocean. Precipitation that drains on the east side heads toward the Atlantic Ocean. Note that not all the streams and rivers reach their destinations. Some rivers empty into deserts where they seemingly die. In South America, the continental divide is distinguished by the Andes. Interestingly, every continent on Earth with the exception of Antarctica has such a divide.

The continental divide for significant thinking happens between "if I can't" and "if I can." Here, the streams of progress are channeled to the positive side, heading toward the ultimate goal of "I can." The danger is that, even at this point, some of those streams and rivers heading toward a positive result may die in the desert of inaction and inertia.

The great thing about being in this position is that, even though the switch has not flipped completely, there is a decided swing in thinking away from "I can't." Now you have something on which to build. The move from "if I can't" to "if I can" is truly significant. "If I can't" sees the negative aspects of not flipping the switch. And while that is important and certainly more desirable than flatly saying "I can't," it is still looking at the negative side of the watershed. From this point forward, it is reflective thinking that wins the day.

I strongly believe that it is important to bring to the front of your mind this fact: *the streams of your life eventually become the rivers of your life.*

The direction in which those streams flow can largely be channeled by your choices. Sure, some things that were not of your choosing have happened to you. Yet it is up to you to decide if you will allow your thinking about those issues to become reactive thinking streams or reflective thinking streams.

"If I can" thinking at least allows for reflective thinking. It will allow your mind to entertain the idea that something beyond the present situation may be possible.

At this point, you may not be able to completely embrace "I can" because you are still in the moonlight. You cannot see clearly that daylight is coming, because the shadows of doubt still linger. But you are moving in the right direction toward truly significant thinking!

Some people assert that they have difficulty moving toward a more fulfilling lifestyle because they have already made some bad decisions. Those may be anything that the individual feels was a bad decision: recreational drug use, a bad choice in a marriage partner compounded by more bad choices after the wedding, unwise financial decisions, or other so-called screw-ups. Such events in life need to be seen in the rearview mirror. Accept them, own them, but then let them go.

Bad decision streams can absolutely compound until they become one of those rivers that you don't want to float down. "If I can" statements about those decisions in your history give you enough moonlight to begin seeing your situation in a different perspective. After you have owned the mistakes of your past, stop talking about your past in reactive ways that hold you back.

"I have two DUIs on my record, so that's going to eliminate any real jobs that I might want."

No. Maybe you shouldn't apply to get your pilot's license with the hope of working for United Airlines. But you can own that historically bad judgment in your life and look at the possibilities *ahead* of you. Start thinking in reflective ways.

"*If I can* be honest with any potential employer and become proactive about my history, and *if I can* demonstrate a sincere life change, maybe *I can* get a job that makes me feel good about myself!"

"I can't"—and to a lesser degree, "if I can't"—life statements build a strong case for inertia and the urge to remain in failure and continue in personal dissatisfaction. I don't know anyone who chooses to verbally state such an attitude. The way it is usually stated is not so much with words as it is with action, or the lack thereof. It could be argued that lack of action is in itself a type of action. Lack of action diminishes the individual's situation, because it furthers the state of inertia. Inertia in thinking is as hard to overcome as it is in the physical sense.

By contrast, "if I can" is that part of significant thinking that begins to move the switch in the right direction, tentative as it may be. Often you will hear someone say something like, "*If I can* get a raise/get a better job/have a happier marriage/go back to school, *then* I will…" The fulcrum of the whole statement is "then." Overcoming inertia in thinking moves the individual beyond the fulcrum to the placement of more weight on what comes after "then."

Most of us will catch ourselves saying things like "if I can…" for one big reason. Saying *if* gives us an escape. It's basically saying, "I'm looking toward the horizon and better things. This is what I want to do with my life, but really, it may not happen, and I don't want to get my hopes up too high."

Yes, life has contingencies that come to bear upon many of our plans. This saying is noteworthy: "If you want to make God laugh, tell God your plans for tomorrow." That's a bit cynical, but it does point out the fact that every breath taken is no promise of another. However, the *if* is included in our statements because we have gotten the idea somewhere that if we flip the switch too much and get too excited about the future, it may not happen.

To at least get to the point in significant thinking that allows you to entertain the thought "Well, *what if* I can..." begins to open your mind to possibilities. One of the ways that happens is when you not only say "*what if* I can" but also begin to visualize what that would look like. Then, it becomes more exciting! To be locked in the cage of "I can't" or even in "what if I can't" is like giving someone else, some situation or some entity, the keys to your mind, your life, and your soul.

In the Eastern and Middle Eastern parts of the world, numerous countries are in turmoil because citizens have been suppressed for a very long time. Some of those countries' governments have been overthrown: some through more or less peaceful means and some through violent revolutions that have caused a lot of bloodshed. Whether it is an individual or a whole society, no one likes to be caged, either mentally or physically or both. Eventually, the yearning to self-determine becomes stronger than the ability to do nothing and acquiesce in captivity.

It's the same with any individual. The person holding the key to your captivity may be another person, a situation, or even yourself.

While moonlight can be beautiful to see, it is not a comfortable situation in which to do things that require more illumination. If you plan to drive from your house to the mall, it would be difficult, dangerous, and illegal to do so by moonlight. No, you would certainly turn on your headlights. But some personalities find themselves undertaking serious life situations while they are still in the moonlight stage of trying to figure it all out.

Illumination given by moonlight varies greatly depending on the lunar cycle. Even the full moon typically provides only about two-tenths lux illumination, a standard measure of luminosity. Under certain weather and geographic conditions, illumination can increase to one lux. Consider that a good level of lighting for reading is somewhere around *five hundred* lux. At peak illuminations, the moon is about five hundred thousand times fainter than the sun.

I use those facts to illuminate the idea that even though you may feel like you are living in moonlight, you still have light! In coaching individuals who feel stuck in their efforts to flip the switch toward "if I can" and eventually toward "I can," I often suggest to them that people have to move forward with the light they have at the moment.

Even though life may seem dim and a situation may seem impossible, there is light. The question to be asked is, "What do you see in the light that you have?" In other words, life has not left you totally blinded to your situation. Instead of concentrating on the darkness, what *can* you identify about your life? What *can* you identify as possible, attainable steps forward?

...

Kyle Crum's Story

Kyle Crum summed up his perspective on life very well: "I am alive for a reason."

I met Kyle when he was the receiving host at a restaurant in Arizona where my wife and I dined. He was twenty-three years old and genuinely liked where he worked. I asked him, "What do you like about working here?"

His reply was quick and heartfelt. "I love the people I meet and the people I work with. I couldn't ask for more!"

Kyle didn't yet see himself as being one of those people who had arrived at some pinnacle of achievement. He was working on that. But he definitely saw himself as having the ability to achieve whatever he set out to do. Part of flipping his switch was deciding what he wanted to do with his life.

He was a very charming young man with a slender build, brown hair, and brown eyes. During my interviews with him at a coffeehouse, I noticed that he had a quick and easy smile that seemed to serve him well when meeting people and making friends. He was outgoing and very approachable. His demeanor was that of an intelligent, laid-back, alert person.

Kyle's family relationships, however, were very fractured according to his descriptions of them. His family consisted of his mother, an adult sister, an older brother, a stepfather who antagonized him at every opportunity, and a younger stepsister. His older biological brother and sister lived in

Indiana, while his mother, stepsister, and stepfather lived in Arizona.

Kyle had encountered so many close calls in life. When his mother was pregnant with him, she skidded on black ice while driving near Indianapolis, which resulted in a very bad accident. Her spine was crushed in four spots. Therefore, she had been on social security disability ever since the accident thanks to rods in her back and her lack of mobility. Also, Kyle was severely injured in the womb during the accident. At Methodist Hospital in Indianapolis, Kyle's mother was told that he probably would not live due to his injuries. It was believed that if he *did* survive his prenatal injuries, he would likely be in a vegetative state the rest of his life. Kyle ended up surviving birth without most of the expected devastating results.

With a broad smile and quick wit, Kyle proudly proclaimed that he had proved them wrong—"God must have a purpose for my life!" Kyle had been deaf until about age five as a result of the head injuries from the prenatal trauma, and he initially had some speech issues. One of his greatest fears was that his earlier hearing loss could still cause his voice to sound abnormal, even though he now had almost 100 percent hearing ability. As Kyle talked, there was absolutely no evidence of any speech impediment. Still, it was a fear he constantly worked at overcoming. His outgoing personality enabled him to easily engage in conversation. He was not willing to let his fear keep him from engaging people. He kept that particular switch flipped toward overcoming a potential hindrance.

While in New Mexico on their way to live in Arizona, he and his mother were involved in yet another accident in which their vehicle was upended due to the malfunction of the trailer they were towing. Kyle showed me the scars on his right arm where the pavement had ground his flesh down to the bone, followed by a severe infection.

Kyle remembered that during high school he had often been very depressed, partly due to the situation at home and other events in his life. One of those events that still haunted him was the death of his biological father, a methamphetamine addict, who died without Kyle having ever met him. I suspected that the realization that he would never meet his father made him miss even more what could have been. Kyle finished high school in 2007 and moved into a house with a roommate in order to get away from his stepfather. His relationship with his stepfather had worsened after his stepsister had been born. His relationship with his mother was still strong, however.

During his deep depression and thoughts of suicide, he had had a positive experience. On one of his worst days during his junior year, he was approached by another youth during weight training for a sports activity. At a time when he had really needed something stable in his life, the other person told Kyle that he had seen him at church and wanted to be friends with him. Kyle was baptized at church camp later that summer. This led to another positive influence that was part-time employment at his church as a youth and operations worker and volunteering in the junior high department.

Unfortunately, his depression did return the next summer at camp. With an ironic smile, Kyle related that the theme of the week had been, "No one is meant to be alone." And yet Kyle was alone in a cabin by himself the entire week. As an indication of his self-directed attitude, Kyle had gone through his Bible and researched scriptures that could help him with his depression. His conclusion was "No one is alone with God."

I asked Kyle, "What has been the biggest influence on your life?" He quickly replied that it had been, and still was, his mother.

"She is a strong person and has been through a lot, but she still manages to be a good person and to love me." He referred to his mother in those terms several times.

Kyle believed that most of his problems centered on procrastination.

"I am a procrastinator, but I'm working on it." He wanted to apply for nursing school but had not yet created a solid plan for accomplishing that dream. It was not an intelligence problem. He affirmed that he had not only survived brain damage as a baby, but was rated almost at a genius level of intelligence. "See, God has something for me."

He also related that he had used to smoke pot a lot. But that seemed to be behind him now. He further shared that he'd made the mistake of spending all his inheritance from his father's death on a Ford Expedition that he had wrecked.

As we talked, I was struck by the fact that Kyle never once in three hours blamed anyone or anything for the problems in his life. That was significant. In spite of having no father, an antagonistic stepfather, drug abuse in the family, and no real mentoring, he still had a perspective on life that allowed him to have a positive attitude, a warm and accepting demeanor, and a willingness to be vulnerable and open.

Kyle had had a series of misfortunes that had cost him his jobs. Bad luck in the form of accidents and injuries had plagued him from the womb. He was breaking that cycle by getting back into college and making something of his life. "I'm alive for a reason," he insisted. He needed and wanted a game plan.

Though Kyle loved working at the restaurant as a host, he'd had other jobs. He had worked at several Circle K gas stations, bouncing around from one living arrangement to another. At his current place of employment, there was evidence of his likability everywhere. I noticed that at the restaurant, people lit up when he was around. Even during our conversation at the coffee shop, various people recognized him and greeted him very warmly.

There was a little bit of the unintentional bad boy image to Kyle. He had had a difficult time as he began his life, and some problems had come calling on him since, with him meeting them halfway. Still, there was a great deal of innocence about him. On his right wrist was a prominent tattoo. When he proudly displayed it to me, it was not what I'd expected. It was a scripture reference: John 14:6—"I am the way, the truth, and the life." Another tattoo on the right side of his chest depicting Jesus Christ gave him additional inspiration. Kyle had those placed there as constant reminders that he was not alone and to give him strength to overcome depression and other hard times.

During our second meeting, Kyle revealed that he intended to finish community college and then transfer into nursing school.

"Why do you want to become a nurse?" I asked him.

"I'm fascinated by the human body—how it works, what makes it go wrong, and so forth. I also like helping people. It just intrigues me, so that's what I want to do."

It was my belief that Kyle had what it took to overcome a difficult beginning in his life. Thanks to his perspective on life, his wit and intelligence, and his determination to make his mother proud, he was working to flip the switch in his life toward pathways that *he* chose—an option he had not always had. It was significant that Kyle *knew* he was not yet a diamond. That was part of the excitement of life for him. He was working toward being what he wanted to be and making his life what he wanted it to become.

I agreed to mentor him, and now I coach him along the way when he asks for it. It is hard to be around Kyle and not feel like cheering for him! Kyle is doing some significant thinking processes and moving toward "I can." He is illuminating his life by flipping the switch.

Kyle could have been limited by his difficulties, which began in the womb. He could have declared, "I can't get what I need out of life." Instead, Kyle moved to the thinking state that declares, "*If I can* make enough money to go to college, *if I can* get accepted into nursing school, *if I can* believe in my dreams, then *I can* have a chance to move forward."

Making It Personal

1. **Identify one area in your life that is not the way you would like it to be.**
2. **Having identified it, what light do you have right now that can be focused on that troublesome area?** For example, perhaps you wish you could take some courses in an area of interest but don't feel like you have the time due to your workload. Shine some light on that area by honestly identifying some potential solutions. Perhaps you could take one course at a time, attend evening classes, use vacation time for a minicourse, work a flexible schedule, etc.

CHAPTER 6
Significant Thinking Principle #4

*Going toward something is better
than going from something.*
(SIGNIF-**I-CAN**-T)

Remember Georgiana and her decision to move out of her parents' home and truly begin her own life? Georgiana had finally decided that having her own place and her own life was more exciting, if somewhat scarier, than staying the way she was. Georgiana found it much more fulfilling to go *to* something (a future on her own) than to go *from* something (the depression of living at home). That is truly significant thinking! It requires a change in perspective.

Understandably, there are times when it is warranted to simply get out the best way you can. In a situation where your own life and health, or that of those who depend on you, are at risk is just one example.

However, a huge part of going to something rather than from something is the ability to be an autonomous adult. Volumes have been written about the definition of an adult. Society is even confused about the whole issue! In some ways, arriving at the age of sixteen and obtaining a driver's license is seen as a big step toward being an adult. Most people would probably agree that it is only a small step toward adulthood and not assurance of mental or emotional maturity.

Some consider eighteen an adult age. After all, one can vote, make his or her own decisions about X-rated material, and even enlist into the military at the risk of being killed. But even with all that, the individual cannot order a glass of wine in a restaurant. At age twenty-one, one can finally do all the previously mentioned things, desirable or not. But is that person still not an adult?

The state of being an adult is not a chronological state. It is not having simply lived long enough that—poof!—you are now an adult because you've reached a certain age. I have known people whom I would not consider adult, even though they were far beyond those ages generally considered adult mileposts. Similarly, I have known teenage persons who were mentally and functionally mature beyond their years.

Basically, an adult is one who is a *self-directed* person. That takes adulthood out of the chronological category and places it into the psychological and emotional ones. In this definition of adulthood, many people find themselves either self-directed in their decisions and choices, or other-directed, in which someone else makes the decisions for them.

A self-directed thinker and decision-maker is a *subscriptive* thinker. They subscribe to thinking through decisions and choices for themselves. Their choices ultimately belong to them. By contrast, the other-directed decision-maker is a *prescriptive* thinker. Their decisions are made or influenced by persons or situations not of their choosing. Other-directed personalities may even know how to make good decisions about their lives and their surroundings, but they allow others to unduly influence them.

Additionally, the true adult thinker will not only direct their own decisions, but they will *take responsibility for them*. The self-directed adult will be oriented toward reflective thinking rather than reactive thinking. "Yes, I made a wrong decision in that situation. But as I reflect upon it, I know what I can do better next time." A solid, balanced adult longs to make good decisions, learn from mistakes, and flip the switch toward a better future. Antonio Harvey is a good example of a self-directed adult.

■ ■ ■

Antonio Harvey's Story

Antonio Harvey retired from the Portland Trail Blazers as an NBA professional basketball player in 2002. He is now an announcer and commentator for the Blazers. He comes from quite an impressive family of pro players. His brother,

Richard, played in the NFL for Buffalo, New England, and the Raiders. His father played in the NFL for Philadelphia, New Orleans, and the Rams.

Antonio is an impressive man even before he opens his mouth to speak, but his thoughts and speech give expression and validation to those thoughts of impressiveness.

He is a man who projects confidence without arrogance, which in itself is an impressive trait in anyone. His confidence impresses me by the very fact that it also projects openness, genuineness, and an appropriate amount of humility. He is one of the few people to whom I must literally look up to. His handshake engulfs my hand! It is also remarkable that he gives no impression of trying to overwhelm anyone. That's a trait of confidence and maturity.

Antonio was not always that confident. He began his journey toward confidence when life began for him in Pascagoula, Mississippi, where he was reared in the Roman Catholic faith. Antonio made note that it was a Southern Catholic church. That experience was formative for the character of his youthful days. Later, he became what he termed a disenfranchised church member. While not dropping his affiliation with his church, Antonio opened his mind to other expressions of faith. As he puts it, "I definitely believe in God, but I believe there are other ways to know God other than the Catholic denomination."

While his church days as a youth may have had some influence on him, Antonio gives the biggest bulk of credit to his mother and his grandmother. Those two influences kept him grounded through what he called his dark times. Early in our conversation, Antonio made it clear. "I believe

God has a greater purpose for my life, because I have been rescued too many times not to believe that." Antonio has a sense of purpose for his life beyond playing for the NBA.

As part of his self-awareness, Antonio realized that being the middle child in his family tended to put him in a position that was not always comfortable for him. It usually meant that he often was too old for some things and too young for others. His younger and older siblings seemed to get most of the attention. He yearned for attention and did things to get it. His parents had divorced, and Antonio grew up in a single-parent household. Most of the time his father was out of his life, partly due to his professional life in the NFL.

Antonio typifies much of his life growing up in Mississippi as being very good, especially his home life and the support of his mother. However, as for his school life, he classifies it as "not so great." Looking in the rearview mirror, he relates that he had been smart but not motivated. Just before his high school senior year, he realized that if he didn't get his grades up to college basketball requirements, he would not be able to play collegiate ball. Motivation had been triggered. He received straight As during his senior year and met the collegiate academic qualifications. With no small amount of pride, Antonio points to the fact that he made the second highest ACT score in his graduating class, a tremendous achievement.

Antonio had been able to flip the switch from mediocre academic status to straight As during his senior year for a very good reason. His perspective on his grades had been transformed to the point of enabling him to be a self-directed person. He had moved from knowing he *should* have better grades to actually achieving them. *Should* doesn't always get it done. It wasn't until his perspective on his grades became a means to an end that he flipped the switch and actually achieved the grades he needed to qualify to play college basketball.

Antonio had begun playing "serious" basketball in the ninth grade. His love of the sport bumped up a huge notch when he went to a basketball camp and, as he says, "I killed it!" He did so well he immediately appeared on the radar of six schools across the country, all before his senior year of high school.

Antonio has a very good description of his own flipping of the switch. For him, the switch had still not been completely flipped to the "on" position.

"At that time, the lights flickered before coming on. For me, it was not a complete flip of the switch," he contends.

Justice for others is a part of Antonio's mind-set. An incident happened during a basketball practice session in his senior year that helped focus his desire for selfless justice. The coach had made an inappropriate comment to another player. Antonio had stepped forward and confronted the coach about the comment. Later, the athletic director told Antonio that he would never get anywhere with "that kind of attitude." Antonio subsequently had to apologize to the coach for confronting him in front of the other players, but he still contended that he had been correct about the inappropriateness of the comment toward the other player. A real level of maturity had been demonstrated that made the protégé the teacher!

You get a glimpse of Antonio's personality and his take on life if you understand this revealing statement from him: "Dark times are hard for me to remember because I have a happy disposition."

One of those dark times for him happened during his freshman year of college. Antonio had begun his collegiate career at the University of Georgia. In spite of his skill with a basketball and his desire to succeed academically, Antonio flunked out. (I can relate!) His mom sat him down and got to the core of the situation when she emphatically asked him, "Now what?"

Antonio says that his mother put *him* in the position to figure out his next moves. The flickers continued.

He was later admitted to Pfeiffer University in Charlotte, North Carolina. By this time, he admits that he had a bit of a chip on his shoulder. A formative time for him began during the first five minutes of his first basketball practice. As Antonio began the drills, the coach told him two words: "Get out!" (Again, I can relate!) No explanation, no qualifying remarks. Nothing but "Get out!"

The next day of practice, the same thing happened. The coach told Antonio, "Get out!" On the third day, there was another infraction of some kind. Again, he was told to "Get out!" Antonio relates that he *finally* got the message. He was to do things the coach's way or not play at all. Period. He admits that the coach had been stripping him down, taking off the layers of attitude in order to get to the good player beneath.

At last, the middle child was getting the attention he wanted and needed. Antonio was successful at basketball, but he also learned to balance his achievements with maturity. He graduated from Pfeiffer University with a bachelor of arts in sociology with a minor in psychology. During that time, the flickering became less, and he began moving toward a steadiness in his life's attitude. He relates with conviction, "It began to happen for me then. If I could go back and change anything, there's nothing I would change. In high school I was an angry child, but I never knew why. I'm not angry anymore."

His professional career in the NBA began in Los Angeles. From there he played in five countries and loved it. Antonio played for the Portland Trail Blazers from 1999 to 2001. He retired from professional basketball to spend time with his wife and children, to whom he was tremendously devoted. Antonio did not want to be away from his children as his father was absent from him.

Throughout our time together, Antonio emphasized his conviction that God had something more for his life. His quiet but persistent search for that something helped Antonio open his mind to lots of possibilities. There is a restlessness that forces Antonio to yet again flip the switch toward new thinking and new possibilities. He is excited about that flip as a chance to give back and be a positive influence in the lives of others, particularly young people.

Antonio has some very interesting ideas about life, child-rearing, drive, and determination. For example, he doesn't believe in having a plan B. In Antonio's thinking, one must drive toward the success that is desired. If there is a plan B, perhaps not all energy to move forward will be put into plan A. If there is a roadblock, and there have been many in his life, you deal with it and move on. Many people would be uncomfortable with that idea and would want to anticipate contingencies. Antonio simply goes full bore toward his goals in spite of potential roadblocks.

At times it could have been easy for him to blame others for some of the roadblocks. His view is that, yes, sometimes people placed obstacles in his life over which he had no control. Yet it was up to him to deal with those hindrances and find a way to overcome them, rather than letting them overcome him.

At other times, he caused his own roadblocks. He relates one that happened when he was much younger. I was somewhat shocked when he told me he'd once been shot with a handgun. His take on it was, "I shouldn't have been there to begin with."

He owned it. He took responsibility for it. And in doing so, he had again flipped a personal switch by deciding to take another route in his life.

"It was my ultimate responsibility," he asserted. "What led me to that event, how I got myself into that situation, was my own choice."

Antonio drew an illustration for me that seemed to encapsulate his philosophy of how to handle life. "Always keep moving." That's his motto. Antonio drew a straight line on a note pad. At intervals on that line were black boxes representing roadblocks. He then actually named each of those roadblocks as a means of being specific about owning the responsibility for his life's direction. Next, he drew pathways around the hindrances and became specific about how he overcame them.

One of the most impressive aspects of Antonio Harvey is his sense of being grounded. He is grounded in faith, in family, and in selflessness. He contends that he has been flipping switches all his life. It hasn't been one big flip. Rather, there have been a number of times in his life when he has had to flip the switch yet again.

Antonio has an insightful way of outlining his philosophy of grappling with life.

"A smart person understands, a learned person is teachable, and a genius knows how to put it all together."

It is a great summary and a wonderful life view.

■ ■ ■

Not everyone begins his or her journey toward fulfillment at "I can't." Maybe your journey starts at "if I can't" or even "if I can." You must decide where you are on the continuum between "I can't" and "I can" in relation to your own target—a target that will help you feel more comfortable in your own skin even *before* you reach it. The very reality of being on the way toward your target, the very act of moving toward something worthwhile, is richly rewarding and energizing.

I recall those first good grades I earned after returning to college. I realized that, no, I had not yet earned my degree. That was yet to be realized in the future. But for the present, I had been infused with a sense of "I *can* do this." My dreams and my sense of worth were on the pathway toward becoming vindicated. I had flipped the switch.

A one-liner by Henry Ford is on target.

"Whether you think you can or you think you can't, you are right."

Making It Personal

1. **Write down a specific area of your life where you feel improvement should happen.** For example, perhaps you will write that public speaking has always been intimidating for you. Or you may write that a broken relationship that has not been reestablished still bothers you. Perhaps finances are a problem. Whatever you want to write, slow down, think about it, and then write.
2. **Now, identify how close you honestly and realistically are to being able to say "I can!" work on *those* areas.** It's not even about solving them immediately. But it *is* about asking yourself how close you are to being able to take some kind of forward action.

CHAPTER 7
Facing Your Fears and Worries

> Not everything that is faced can be changed;
> but nothing can be changed that is not faced.
> —Author Unknown

Walking alone on that cold, dark night in Virginia, my struggle of the soul culminated in an epiphany. It was almost a Frostian moment. Figuratively speaking, I saw two paths on a snowy evening, and I chose the one that has made all the difference in my life.

It was reflective thinking about the chemistry professor who had told me I need not take the final exam and the dean who had told me to get out that had prompted action. My reflective thinking became more intense in the months that followed. I knew in my heart that something had to be done. I just had not been ready for that something until the evening when the switch flipped and my idle thinking became determination. Timing is everything.

The difference between reflective thinking and simply wallowing in misery is that reflective thinking can lead to action. By contrast, reactive thinking is rarely a good thing. Wallowing in failure leads to a victim mentality, viewing life in a negative way, and perhaps placing more importance on a particular failure than is warranted.

Remember when your parents asked if you would jump off a cliff if everybody else was doing it? Some things you don't want to fail at: hang gliding, parachuting, flying an airplane—you can add others. But there are more mundane situations that make people worry about failure.

My wife and I once watched the two-hour documentary *My 600-lb Life*. The subject of the program was a young married woman who had been molested as a child. Her weight gain had continued through childhood and into her adult years, topping out at 653 pounds. Her weight had placed her into a handicapped position, totally dependent on her husband for every aspect of her life, from personal hygiene to even a simple drink of water.

Her doctors stressed that she would die soon if she didn't lose weight...and a lot of it. Reflective thinking about her life led her to take action in the form of reduction surgery, which reduced her stomach to only a fraction of its usual size. She reflected on what had brought her to such a life-threatening situation and was faced with choosing one of two paths: stay in the same condition that would eventually lead to death, or take action by having a surgery that also had significant life-threatening possibilities.

In spite of her deep fears about the surgery, her thought process led her to believe that it was better to face her fears and give herself a chance at a normal life for herself and also for her husband. It turned out that multiple surgeries would be needed over several years to remove fatty skin deposits and overhanging areas resulting from her weight loss. Each surgery brought its fears, but each one was handled with a perspective on life that literally led from inertia to action. As she lost weight over the years, she was overjoyed at being able to move about and do things she had never done in her life.

The point of this story is that fear *can* cause inertia, even to the point of choosing death rather than action. Remember that earlier quote about the pain of doing nothing becoming more unbearable than the fear of doing something? That was surely part of what led this 653-pound woman to move from inertia to action. Sadly, she died from complications related to later surgeries. This courageous woman had flipped the switch, but perhaps she flipped it too late. I have to believe that it was not the flip of the switch that took her life but the delay in flipping it.

I learned a long time ago that personal inertia may very well make you sick. Mine often comes in the form of headaches. I tend to get a headache if there is something that I am not facing and don't want to deal with. At those times, I have to do some reflective thinking and ask myself if my headache is due to something that is bothering me, or if it is truly a nerve and muscle problem. In such situations, an individual will often do one of two things: stay in a state of inertia even while feeling unsettled, unhappy, vaguely queasy, and in need of a sense of direction, or literally get sick of the painful state in which he or she is in and do something to move forward.

To choose the first option requires a payment be made in physical, spiritual, and emotional unrest. Hunger for equilibrium can be an intense motivator toward action. My personal history reveals that, at those times of inertia in the face of unrest and lack of fulfillment, my soul suffered. Yes, there are times when suffering is necessary because we have to wait. But also ask yourself, "Is my waiting and suffering due to my unwillingness to honestly face the cause of my discomfort?" That question is extremely important.

In the event that an individual does not confront the inertia, then often the decision is made for that person. By not deciding, you essentially decide to give your power away to others. By doing nothing in a situation is really making the decision to allow circumstances to take control of you and make the decision for you. When that happens, you are no longer autonomously self-directed but other-directed.

How much better it is to choose the second option! Self-direction allows people to use the personal gifts, talents, choices, and resources available to them to make decisions on behalf of their own interests.

Listen to the things that go bump in your soul. These are the things that can help create inertia. By listening to my fears, I was able to have a sense of urgency that was startling. With crystal clarity, I realized that I was afraid of staying in that awful sense of failure. If I stayed in that state of fearing to fail again, I would always be in that state. If I was to ever move toward the future I wanted, I had to face my fears and return to college. *Not because of the college degree, but because I grew enough to face my failure and fears.* College was not going to make me accomplished, but I had to accomplish college to move on.

Eight Ways to Face Your Fears

Facing your fears is not easy, but naming them and externalizing them is a good thing. It helps you get past them by actually dealing with them.

According to anxiety expert Doug Mennin, PhD, associate professor of psychology at Hunter College in New York City, "When people get better at identifying what they are experiencing—positive or negative—it gives them mental space to process their emotions rather than be controlled by them."

For example, UCLA researchers recruited study participants who were afraid of tarantulas. The volunteers were asked to approach a tarantula in one of four ways: talk about their fear of the tarantula, describe the tarantula in neutral terms, change the subject and talk about something else, or do nothing at all.

It was discovered that those who talked about their fear of the tarantula had a real reduction in their physical symptoms compared to those who chose the other reactive options.

∎ ∎ ∎

Are you living a *fractional-ownership* life? Central to the whole idea of using significant thinking principles to face your fears is the issue of who or what owns you and your destiny. In real estate, there is a term called "fractional ownership." I learned that term from looking at property on the Oregon coast. I saw a real estate listing for a condominium on the beach overlooking the ocean. Boy was it gorgeous! Long stretches of beach both north and south made it very inviting.

I phoned the real estate agent to find out more information. I've almost always believed in the adage "If it sounds too good to be true, it probably is." The agent informed me that the cost listed on the brochure was what in real estate is termed a fractional ownership. You only own a fraction of the condo and share a fraction of the expenses. When I asked how many fractional ownerships were possible, I was told that the property was divided into ten fractional ownerships. Ten? That put the condo at about one million dollars.

The point is, some people live fractional-ownership lives. They are willing to let fear, prejudice, failure, inertia, and a multitude of other issues own parts of their lives. They are not able to have full possession, full self-direction, or full joy in the most productive and purposeful ways possible for them. *You* should get to decide who, what, and which issues will own parts of your life.

Who told you that you should be afraid to try that college course you've been thinking about? Who told you that you aren't smart enough? Who told you that you will never get out of debt? Who told you that you can't live a life that is meaningful and purposeful in the ways that you have longed for? One of the reasons some people don't challenge those affronts to their being is because they are afraid to try.

A huge part of the STPs is facing your fears. Here are eight ways I've laid out to accomplish that:

1. **Identify them.** In facing your fears, it is important to know what they are. Free-floating, nonspecific anxiety may manifest itself in a vague feeling of emotional discomfort. Do some soul-searching, and be honest with yourself. Is there something you have wanted to do but have never taken a step toward? Name it. Write it down. Roll it around in your head. Is there a fear that is holding you back? Do the same thing with the fear. Name it. Write it down. It helps to objectify such things instead of leaving them as vague anxieties.

   For example, maybe you have always wanted to try singing, but you have never actually tried it. Write down that you would like to sing or learn to sing. It doesn't mean you have to audition for a talent show. You might feel more comfortable hiring a voice coach to see if you have talent, and if so, move forward toward developing that talent. If you don't have the talent you thought you might have, at least you will have explored it and learned something about yourself.

2. **Sort out the main issues.** After you have identified your concerns or fears, identify which ones are the most crucial to your moving forward. Which ones are truly related to your satisfaction with life? Which ones are holding you back from getting closer to flipping the switch inside you that turns on your creative significant thinking?

   From your list of concerns and fears, prioritize the ones you think must be tackled first. Some personality types want to tackle all of them at once. Big mistake! Doing that may quickly result in a sense of being overwhelmed, which may transform into a sense of hopelessness and ultimately failure—the opposite of what you are trying to achieve.
3. **Get the facts, not the rumors.** Is what you are hearing through the media really true for your life? Remember—that big screen in your family room is not spelled with a capital T. It's just a television. While much good comes from it, it is not the final word. Have you ever suspected that what the media puts before you sometimes becomes a self-fulfilling prophecy?
4. **Listen to your gut.** The viability of gut instinct can increase with each year of experience and practice. That is not a given, however. To learn to have good instincts about situations, people, and impressions, it is necessary to listen to those instincts. More often than not, my instincts have been correct. Still,

it is always wise to back up instinctive feelings and intuition with some fact-checking. Good instincts for adults come with practice and time.

Children may also have good instincts, but instinctive conditioning comes with age and practice. Even though instinct is not always correct, it should at least prompt you to check where those feelings are coming from and why. The savings in anguish, angst, and anxiety could well make the gut-check worth the trouble. Don't ignore your instincts!

I once hired a person to be on my staff that turned out to be a mistake. I thought I needed someone sooner than later and moved forward to fill the position. My gut instinct about the person, and that of some others, was that the person would not work out. My instincts were that this person was not a team worker and had more self-interest than was good for the organization. Yet on paper it seemed like it would be a good fit. My instincts turned out to be accurate. I should have listened to that sense of uneasiness that said, "Watch out."

5. **Stop the ampersands!** Ampersands are those little & signs that can introduce something negative or something positive into the conversations that you have with yourself. Refuse to allow your fears to become connected and multiplied.

"I'm afraid that such and such will happen & then such and such will happen & then that other thing will happen &..."

Life could easily degenerate into a series of "and then" added one upon the other. Remember Tom? His ampersands were something like this: "I may not get that job & then I'll question my whole professional validity & then the job I have may end & then I may lose my car & then I won't be able to go to interviews & then I'll be seen as a loser without a car & then my family will also suffer because they can't go where they need to & then..."

Tom had to stop the ampersands and concentrate on doing a better job of interviewing. Period. That needed to be his first priority. To stay in this state of being is "worry farming." When one is worry farming, it operates much like any farming. Seeds of doubt and worry are planted. For example, "What if what happened at the Boston marathon terrorist attack should happen to me or to my loved ones? How could I possibly cope?" The seeds of fear and doubt are planted.

Next, those seeds are allowed to become fertilized and nurtured in the recesses of the mind. The fears, rational or otherwise, sprout into enough negative emotional energy to sap the positive energy that can be generated. Instead, to avoid worry farming, look at the positive outcomes of even such horrible tragedies, such as the heroic efforts given without second thought and the outpouring of care and prayer across the world. It serves as a reminder to us that the United States has friends all around the world, not just enemies.

6. **So what?** What is the worst that can happen if this fear comes true? Often it's not as bad as it may seem at first glance on the emotional level. Someone once said that most of the things people worried about in life never happened. That may be the case with most of your fears and concerns. Are you afraid to take a step toward flipping the switch away from fear of failure and toward action? If so, what is the worst that could happen if you begin your journey? Failure? So what? You will definitely fail if you don't try.
7. **Don't run—it'll chase you!** In the event of a bear threat, experts advise people to not turn and run. It will only chase you. It's the same with fears. The more you run from them, the more they will chase you. They won't just go away.
8. **Plan steps toward easing or eliminating the fear.** One of the best ways to do so is to take steps *toward* the fear. For example, if you are afraid of public speaking and feel it is holding you back in your career or life in general, consider taking an introductory course in speech communication. You will not regret it. Add whatever fear is nagging you to the bucket list of things you resolve will not win over you. Instead of fear winning over you, make plans to be the winner over fear.

Darlene's Story

Darlene was afraid to confront her husband about their relationship. It wasn't that he beat her or otherwise physically abused her. The abuse was more subtle, involving a feeling of being seen as inferior in his eyes. She felt put down whenever she had an opinion that was different from his. She also felt that she should not be herself and open up in a discussion because she dared not be wrong about anything that would cause her husband to treat her with disdain, even in front of others.

The more Darlene ignored the situation, the more she felt tense and angry deep down. She was constantly under emotional stress due to the effort needed to keep a lid on her emotions and opinions. She became depressed, and her physical health took a hit too. She became ill with colitis. It was only in consultation with her physician that the issue of *why* she was having so much intestinal trouble surfaced. Suspecting that her discomfort was at least partially anxiety related, he referred her to a therapist. Darlene approached the possibility of seeing a therapist with much initial trepidation, but she was determined to go through with it.

After a few sessions, she began to open up. She shared with the therapist that part of the reason she put up with her husband's browbeating was her fear of losing him.

There was no evidence that he would leave her, yet she had jumped to that conclusion. It's terrible to be lonely alone, but it is even worse to be lonely while with someone.

To condense the story, Darlene was eventually able to tell her husband how she felt, and they began seeing the therapist together. The result was that both Darlene and her husband grew immensely in their insights about themselves, each other, and the ways in which they communicated. The colitis improved.

Making It Personal

1. **What worries you the most?** Is it your past, present, future, or all three?
2. **Why does it worry or concern you?**
3. **What steps will you take to stop worry farming?**
4. **What resources will you use in those steps?**

CHAPTER 8

Consolidate Your Power, Not Your Problems

A big part of significant thinking that leads to flipping the switch is putting your problems and your fears into perspective.

Imagine looking at a bear through a telescope from a distance. (There's that bear again!) It looks even more huge and threatening than it normally is. Now, take away the telescope and look at the bear and how far away he actually is, and you have a much better perspective on just how much of a threat that bear really is to you. It doesn't make the bear go away, nor does it lessen the reality that the bear exists. It does give you the *truth* about what is threatening you. It's the same with problems. Looking at problems through a telescope (if not a microscope) magnifies their significance.

You may do what I call "problem consolidation." For example, when a consumer is having trouble meeting his or her multiple financial obligations, it is sometimes a good financial strategy to obtain a consolidation loan that covers multiple obligations. That loan covers the smaller obligations that are coming from multiple sources. The consolidation loan offers the benefit of one loan rather than, for instance, five loans. The others that may be in arrears can be paid off or brought current, improving your credit score. Often the monthly payment on the consolidation loan is more manageable than the total payments of all the individual ones.

Unfortunately, the idea of consolidating obligations may be carried over to how we deal with stress and anxiety related to problems and hindrances in life. Some personalities tend to consolidate all their problems into one big headache of worry, stress, and even anger. When that happens, the individual makes a big payment on those consolidated problems each day—even every hour of each day. Unlike the loan consolidation, problem consolidation does not have a lower payment. It has a bigger one. When problems are consolidated, payments are made. Below is a list of those responsible for your debts:

1. **Your health.** It is well known that stress and worry will take their toll in the form of headaches, high blood pressure, heart disease, sleeplessness, and more.
2. **Your relationships.** The more mental and spiritual energy spent on consolidated problems, the less is left to be spent on family, friends, career

development, relaxation and fun, and other areas that are considered truly important in life.

3. **Your creativity.** A mind overwhelmed with stress and worry is often one that is not free to put skills, intelligence, and creativity to maximum effectiveness.
4. **Your work performance.** I have always felt that if you have a job to do, do it to the best of your ability. Anyone who has consolidated his or her problems and feels burdened by them will not be able to give maximum performance to the tasks at hand.
5. **Your financial stability.** According to a YouGov.com poll for the Institute of Financial Planning (IFP) and National Savings and Investments (NS&I), approximately two-thirds of people were at least somewhat worried about their finances. The study also revealed that most people were not taking any steps to improve their financial situation. Forty-three percent admitted that they worried about money more often than not. Seventeen percent worried about it all the time. But only 14 percent took any steps to identify the causes of their financial stress and plan accordingly.

Financial stability may be one, or even the biggest, of your problems. However, worrying and fretting over it will not increase your financial stability by one cent. A better approach is to calm yourself, sit down, and write out what your real situation is at the moment. Worry and stress over

> financial matters can actually *decrease* your financial stability because mental energy and creativity are used up by worry, which is unproductive, instead of going to problem solving. Do the problem solving with your spouse or significant other, not alone.

Flipping the switch toward financial stability does not imply that you are suddenly wealthy or will become wealthy. Financial stability applies to everyone, wealthy or not. It simply means that you should take a serious look at your financial situation and decide what steps can be taken to give you the assurance that your resources are not controlling you, but that you are controlling your resources. Basically, it's just good stewardship. Instead of letting worry rob you of a sense of peace, start taking steps that will help you. Consider taking on a second job. Consider downsizing your home. Consider downsizing your lifestyle. This is not easy, but it's better than worry without action.

■ ■ ■

Like most people, I have Microsoft Word on my computer. After opening a Word document, I have the ability to magnify that document by clicking the view tab and selecting the zoom-in option. I can magnify that document even to the point of seeing only one word on a whole page. Suppose I zoom in so close that the only word I see in the whole document is "failure." Further, let's suppose the word "failure" becomes the only word that is significant to me and the only word that I can even think about. Failure is what I am focused on because the word "failure" is all I can see!

Again, I select the view tab and make a selection. But instead of zooming in, I zoom out. By zooming out, I get a better picture of the *context* in which the word "failure" appears. I may discover that the document is not emphasizing failure at all, but instead reveals "Do not let your failure define you."

Now I have a context into which the word "failure" can be placed, and it isn't the same context as I originally thought. It's exactly the opposite! At first glance, I gave the word too much significance to the point that it obscured the real meaning of the document.

One evening, while driving from eastern Oregon to Portland, I was very preoccupied with a problem in a conflict resolution situation. I was working with a group of people who were in deep conflict. Why do these people not get along? Why can't they see each other's point of view during the sessions without so much vitriolic attitude toward one another? During the three-hour drive home, I kept turning the problem over and over in my mind, looking at the situation in which the group found itself.

As I neared Portland, I came upon a transport truck with a large bumper sticker that warned, "Back off!" I wasn't tailgating, but the driver must have put the message on his truck to warn anyone across the country that he took a dim view of vehicles he couldn't see, pun intended. As I stared at the sticker and wondered about the history of the driver, it finally struck me that I was missing two important aspects of the conflict resolution situation.

First, I was not dealing with a group of people, but two groups of people, each with its own ideology and views. As the conflict heated up, both sides became so zoomed in on their positions that they couldn't see anything *but* their own positions. Both sides had become so blinded by the possibility of failing to win that neither of the two sides could look forward to anything but failure of the whole group.

The second realization was that I was dealing with the histories of about fifteen people. To see them as one organism was a mistake. What needed to happen was to interview each of the individuals privately and confidentially to get beneath the surface of the expressed discomfort. When I did that, it revealed issues in the histories of those individuals that were not always related to the *expressed* reasons of why we were having the sessions. A question toward the end of each private conversation helped. The question was "Given what you have shared with me about your life and your history, how do *you* think your background is impacting your feelings in the larger group?" It was discovered that individual history had a very profound impact on current ways of functioning and relating to others.

As I helped the group zoom out and take a look at the larger picture, their relationships and problem-solving abilities improved immensely. Again, consolidate your power, not your problems.

Significant thinking can enable individuals to put problems and failures into the proper context. Having done that, a path for the future is now coming into view. A part of putting problems into context is deciding that you will not give them a payday. That is, *you* decide that the payments on problems come at the cost of your power. Why is it that we give away our power to our problems when we could use that power to have a better life and more peace of mind? Perhaps we do that because we don't feel like we have much power, if any. Fortunately, we *do* have power!

The late Howard Y. McClusky, a professor of educational psychology at the University of Michigan, espoused a simple yet insightful way of expressing the relationship between power, problems, and quality of life. Called the theory of margin, it is expressed as a simple equation that helps individuals visualize the relationship between power, load, and the margin between the two.

$$M = L/P$$

The equation expresses visually what everyone deals with on a daily basis. L represents one's load of problems and stressors. P represents the power or resources one has to carry that load. M represents the margin or difference between the load and the power needed to carry it. The more power one has to carry the load, the greater the emotional and physical margin between the two. The greater the margin, the greater the possibility of a healthy emotional state.

Whether expressed in McClusky's equation or by some other means, it is the margin between resources and problems that gives adults either a sense of consolidated power or a sense of consolidated problems. Some of the load factors for adults may include career development issues, financial stress, internal struggles with unresolved personal issues, family responsibilities, addiction, socioeconomic status, and many others. Add those issues to the constant communication and connectivity to which most of us are tethered, and the load factors just keep getting heavier and more significant. All are hindrances to flipping the switch unless there is sufficient margin between the load factors and the power to carry them.

For an adult to flip the switch from inertia to forward movement, it is often necessary to use the zoom-out option, look at his or her load, the power to carry it, and the margin between the two. Trouble is at the doorstep when the load is equal to the power to carry it. When the load is more than the power to carry it, trouble is shaking hands with you! Physical and emotional distress is sure to follow if this condition is prolonged.

Making It Personal

1. **Do some reflective thinking by finishing these two sentences.**

    The five biggest load factors in my life are:

    a.
    b.
    c.
    d.
    e.

    The five biggest strengths to support those factors are:

    a.
    b.
    c.
    d.
    e.

2. **Therefore, my margin is:**

    a. High
    b. Narrow
    c. In deficit

3. If you chose b or c, how will you increase or maintain your margin?

    a. Decrease the load
    b. Increase the emotional and physical strength needed
    c. Do nothing

CHAPTER 9

Four Aspects of Problems

What is the best method for confronting problems? It's usually not as simple as asking, "What's your problem?" As with fears addressed earlier, most of us find that we often have more than one problem or load factor.

Just as we did with fears, begin by writing them down. Write down what is bothering you as best as you can articulate it. I promise this will help! This is important, because writing them down will help move you from internalization of the problems to externalization of them. When there are more than one, write all of them down as they hit your mind. Keep a note pad and pen handy. If you prefer, use a computer. But make sure you print out what you wrote so that you avoid reinternalizing it to a machine that will conveniently hide it for you! The important part is actually forming the words that best express the summation of the problems.

For example, when I was teaching graduate school at Ball State University, I would at times feel overwhelmed. In addition to teaching, I had another demanding job, a family, issues with my parents' health, and just the stresses of life in general. I began writing out sentences, phrases, and sometimes just reminders. As I continued to do that, three amazing things began to happen:

1. I discovered that the more I wrote about what was causing me distress, the more *clarity* I had about myself and my situation. There is much value in writing out a difficult situation. It gradually causes mental abilities to become fluid where they were once frozen. A clearer and perhaps more accurate picture of the real situation emerges as the mind is freed to think.

    This type of externalization is a good thing to do at night. Just before turning out the light, write out what you must deal with the next day. Additionally, write out possible solutions, or at least steps to take toward some relief and a time line for those steps. Your night's rest will probably be more rewarding because you have done all you can at that time, and your brain knows it!

2. As I gained more clarity about the situation, I began to see things in a different *light*. Writing out a synopsis of the situation not only brings needed clarity, it will also allow mental abilities to be directed onto *pathways of action* that may be taken toward the problem's solution. It may be unrealistic

to expect that the problem will be easily alleviated. Outlining steps toward a solution and *actually* taking action on those steps is essential to flipping the switch from despair and anger toward hope and resolution.

3. Gaining clarity and outlining pathways toward action gives me a sense of *peace*. Peace comes from knowing the problem has been faced with clarity, it has become externalized, and pathways toward solutions are more promising than previously thought. Hopelessness and free-floating anxiety are gradually replaced by a sense of direction, hopefulness, and purpose.

It's all a part of flipping your unique mental and emotional switch from inertia to progress that leads to a more fulfilling life. In summary, don't pay your problems to live inside your head. Get them out and onto paper, externalize them, and begin forming a pathway toward progress.

■ ■ ■

Let's talk about gaining personal power. I've said it is optimal to consolidate your power, not your problems. But how does that happen? Most people have more power than they realize. The significance of power in one's life is not always measured by physical strength but by *strength that enables one to face weaknesses*. At times it is truly strength measured *by* weakness. I have seen more personal growth from individuals who can honestly admit to weakness in particular areas than I have seen in individuals who seem to already know it all—or would have the world believe they do.

In that regard, following this axiom is good advice. (Frame it!)

> Not everything that is faced can be changed;
> but nothing can be changed that is not faced.

There is no more deceitful mirror than the one we look into alone. That's why it is often valuable and personally helpful to have others assist you in obtaining a truer picture of yourself, your situation, and your power to deal with it all. Everyone can benefit from an objective point of view in life—someone who will be honest and candid, yet someone who can be trusted with your thoughts, hopes, and fears.

■ ■ ■

Dr. Richard Hughes's Story

When I lived in Indiana, I had a friend who was an excellent veterinarian. Richard was a very kind and insightful man with an uncanny connection with animals. One day while we were having lunch in a restaurant, I happened to mention to him that another friend, whom I'd spotted at a distant table, was going through a really difficult time with his dog and was considering putting the animal down. Richard said nothing about my statement at that moment.

When we finished lunch, he asked me to introduce him to this friend. I did, and Richard asked him for more information about the dog and what behavior it was demonstrating. We learned that the dog would not move, would barely eat or drink, would not interact with anyone, and was totally depressed almost to the point of being catatonic. Richard asked, "May I come by and examine the dog?" His reputation was so well known that we quickly received permission.

As we entered the backyard of the dog owner's home, I thought, "Wow, that dog is going to chew us up and not bat an eye." The dog also had a reputation—especially with me, and it wasn't a good one! Absolutely no one but the owner ever dared come near that dog's yard or house. I was not feeling comfortable to say the least.

But there was the dog. Quiet. Unmoving. Eyes mostly closed. I briefly thought he was already dead and I might escape his wrath, but he was still alive. Gently and bravely, Richard knelt beside the dog and did an assessment of the animal's condition.

Eventually he stood and told the owner that, as far as he could tell, there were no obvious physical ailments that would warrant the dog being in such a malaise.

"Has anything happened around here that has upset your dog?" he asked.

The owner replied quietly, "Well, yes, he began acting this way about a week after my wife, Faye, passed away a month ago."

A light dawned in Richard's eyes.

"If I owned this dog, I wouldn't put him down. He's in grief crisis. He's lost, and *he's just trying to find his way*," he explained.

I have never forgotten those words. I have used them for myself, and I have used them in coaching others. Please never give up on yourself moving forward, not even on your most discouraging days. Remember that you are trying to find your way. Sometimes people are simply searching for the power they need to find their way forward. That may be your frame of mind as you read this book.

■ ■ ■

I enjoy reading western novels, especially those based on historical research. In Louis L'Amour's *The Strong Shall Live*, the following quote caught my mind.

> They tell us, Sir, that we are weak, unable to cope with so formidable an adversary. But when shall we be stronger? Will it be next week? Will it be next year? Will it be when we are totally disarmed and a guard stationed in every house? Shall we gather strength by irresolution and inaction? Sir, we are not weak if we make proper use of those means which…nature has placed in our power (L'Amour 1981).

This is what I like to call "strengthening your hand." Please understand that in discussing strengthening your hand, I am not talking about power that is at the expense of others. *Grasping power is not power*—rather, it is breaking off a piece of the island for yourself that leaves others diminished. The power each person needs is that which helps him or her become stronger and more confident in moving from inertia to purpose and achievement. When you come to that place of personal power, reach back your hand and lift up someone else.

Know that the end does not always justify the means. For example, look at the power used by many political candidates. It would appear that the power of slander, innuendo, half-truths, hatefulness, and greed is fair and acceptable for use against other candidates under the guise that, in the long run, "it is best for the American people." Such self-delusional and self-aggrandizing statements become an ambrosia that makes it all taste so much better.

Part of the oath that physicians take is that they will do no harm. Power that raises you up and gives a positive image in the rearview mirror of your life after you receive it is good power! This is what I mean by strengthening your hand. It is not strengthening your hand against others, but simply adding to *your* hand those things that help *you* find your way toward flipping the switch. There are five fingers on that hand. I was tempted to be mischievous and call it the "digital approach."

Finger One: When you're hot, you're hot—when you're not, you're not. Knowing your limitations is a good thing. The *American Idol* television series is a good example of that. Some of the contestants truly believe that they are not only good singers, but that they are good enough to win the competition. Some are heartbroken when they are rejected.

It's sad when someone thinks he or she is very good at something when it is painfully obvious that he is not good at it, whether it is singing, art, sports, or something else. And just as sad is the fact that most people won't break the news to that person! They'll just let him go on unaware of the truth. There isn't an *American Idol* judges panel for everyone (although that might not be a bad idea).

So do it yourself. Discover those aspects of your abilities that are appropriate for you. That is, those abilities you possess that help you move forward in life in a positive way. It could be your personality, your skills at certain tasks, your organizational abilities, or maybe a forgiving attitude. Everyone has something, so find out which ones you possess. These are sometimes referred to as one's cutting edges. They help you cut through life's situations in ways that have a positive impact on you and on those with whom you interact.

And just as important, discover your growing edges. They are aspects of your life that are not quite at the level you would prefer, but could be sharpened to the point that they too become cutting edges for you. Perhaps some people perceive you as rude or unapproachable due to your shyness. Maybe you are not good at managing money. Or maybe you aren't able to maintain intimate relationships with those close to you. Those are just examples. You need to articulate your own growing edges so that you can grow in those aspects of your life.

Not long ago, I took up golf. Or maybe I should say it took me! The first time I played happened to be with people who were fairly skilled at it. It was an impromptu game. I didn't have a glove, I didn't have decent clubs, and I didn't know the rules. By the time I had finished the tenth hole, my left palm was purple with bruises! I had held the club in a death grip, because surely if I strangled the darn thing into submission and took up chunks of turf big enough to plant an elephant, I would do better. My game stunk so badly that it left an odor on the course! I knew I should have just quit and let the others finish. That would have made more sense to the game than I possessed at that time.

In the last couple of years I have gotten better—not good, but better. What helped was a realistic evaluation of my abilities, leading me to pay for a few lessons. I know I will never join the PGA Tour, and I don't really want that. But I have improved from that first game.

The point is that unless you are willing to be vulnerable and mature enough to find out your abilities and weaknesses, as well as your strengths and potential, you will be handicapped in flipping the switch toward a more fulfilling life.

Finger Two: Have a coach blow the whistle on you.
Find a life coach and work out an agreement with that person to coach you through the process of identifying some of your strengths and weaknesses. Again, a combination approach is best, using testing, consultation, goal clarification, and whatever other resources that help move you forward.

Make sure the coach you choose has your best interests in mind. I suggest you interview the person to determine his or her expertise, education, experience, listening skills, and attitude. A life coach does not have to be medically trained, but he or she should have the education and training for being a life coach. In my own case, I have an earned doctorate in adult and community development, with a cognate in business along with postdoctoral continuing education and experience in coaching adults. Someone else may not have a doctorate in a related field, but he or she may have certifications in coaching, along with experience.

My first session with clients is focused on getting to know them and understanding what it is they need from a life coach. Equally important, I want them to understand who I am and my background, education, and experience. It is extremely important that the two of you have good chemistry in order for the relationship to work. If there is a lack of mutual respect and openness between coach and client, then the communication may suffer and progress may be curtailed.

Your coach needs to have the courage to offer new and insightful ideas to help you flip the switch. These insights may be different from the ones you have in mind. Similarly, he or she may need to push you a bit toward decision-making, exploration, alternative pathways toward action, giving up some hindrances, and other clarifications. Together, you are planning a course of action and then moving forward with that plan.

The early stages of your relationship with your life coach or mentor may be focused on building a relationship and designing a pathway forward for your life situation. Later, that relationship may shift more toward mentoring you *along* the pathway. I don't advocate that you feel totally comfortable with your coach in the sense that you are never challenged. Instead, ask yourself if you have a sense of confidence in your coach. If not, find another coach.

Finally, give yourself to the process of working with a coach. Allow the coach to safely get inside your head and heart. That is, work at being open in a way that allows the coach to help you the most. If you are reluctant to share what is on your mind, your coach's abilities to assist you will be handicapped. If at any time you feel uncomfortable for any reason, stop, share your feelings honestly and openly, find the source of your discomfort, and resolve it or terminate the relationship.

Finger Three: Seek divine help. I would be remiss if I did not mention to you a source that has been powerful and helpful to me through the years. Yes, it's a very personal consideration. If you are a person of faith, how have you used your faith and your faith resources to give you a sense of strength and resilience?

One does not have to be religious to be spiritual. Faith and spirituality, and how you use them, are unique to you. Religion, on the other hand, is how you express your spirituality. Often people overlook that resource, thinking that it does not apply to them because they are not "religious." Religion gets a bad rap sometimes. But religion is simply one's external life response to one's internal faith. Truly, faith without works is dead.

If you are a person of faith, you may want to consult with your minister, rabbi, priest, or other spiritual leader in addition to your life coach and enlist his or her support. Sometimes a spiritual leader is trained and experienced as a life coach. However, do not assume that such is the case. It does not always follow that a leader who is trained in theology also has the ability to assist you in flipping the switch and moving forward.

Finger Four: Get your family involved. Get your family behind you as you work your way through tough times. Even in good times, family can be helpful in determining the next steps in your life. As long as the power dynamics of a family are balanced and sensitively shared, family input and support can be invaluable. If your family is not supportive, remember that not all family is biological. Not all family dynamics happen inside a biological family. There may be people in your life who could very appropriately walk beside you during your journey and lend aid and support.

Finger Five: Get grounded. Emotions can be like a handful of balloons being released at the same time. They all fly off at once and in different directions. Ask yourself, "What is the *purpose* of what I am doing right now?" If the answer is not one that helps move you forward but only adds to the fragmented nature of your life, then it needs to be reexamined.

A part of being grounded is deciding that some aspects of your life need to be addressed. Deciding to decide is a big part of the process. It is the first step on the pathway to flipping the switch and moving forward.

Making It Personal

1. **What are some of the challenges facing you?** (Examples: financial concerns, health issues, child-rearing challenges, employment, etc.)
2. **How am I dealing with the fears associated with those problems?** (Examples: avoidance, denial, overthinking without action, etc.)
3. **What will I do about those problems and fears today, tomorrow, and the day after that?**
4. **Choose someone or a group to hold you accountable both for taking action and not taking action.**

CHAPTER 10
Personal Perspective and Attitude

Attitude is a choice but not always an instantaneous one. Attitude is greatly influenced by perspective. In my case, it was a sudden realization that I could either be acted upon or I could take control of my attitude. That perspective on my situation—the way in which I looked at it—allowed me to change my attitude. Just saying that I could become an "I can" person would be like water off a duck's back without having a change in my perspective. It just wouldn't soak in. It helped me change my attitude from being a victim of "I can't succeed at college" to that of growing up, becoming determined, and making plans to move beyond my situation.

■ ■ ■

Sean Ludeman's Story

A wonderful example of someone who has *attained* an excellent personal perspective and attitude is Sean Ludeman. I emphasize the word "attained" because often it does take effort and pain to gain an authentic and healing personal perspective against odds that you did not create.

I first met Sean at a Barnes & Noble bookstore where he was an employee. Two things about him became immediately apparent. One was the intelligence that shone through his eyes. Sean's eyes were bright and alert, showing a type of intelligence that, rather than being cold and off-putting, drew you to him.

The other feature was his personality. I was in the bookstore to find help with publishing. Should I go the almost-impossible traditional route of book publishing? Should I do e-publishing? Should I do a combination of both? The bookstore manager was trying to be helpful, but she was not succeeding. To help usually involves listening.

"Your best option today is e-publishing," she told me. Sean overheard the conversation and, looking up from his own work, agreed with the manager. But the big difference is *how* he agreed with her. It was in a manner and attitude that in effect said, "Yes, by all means do the e-publishing. But there's more to the story."

He later emphasized trying both traditional and e-publishing. The way Sean handled that situation told me that I really needed to sit down with him and pick his brain. In later conversations with him, Sean was very encouraging about the book, how to publish it, the book's cover, fresh ideas, and more. Each time we met, Sean's personality was always uplifting and encouraging.

Sean was more than intelligent eyes and personality. Although, those two things served as unspoken words that said it was all right to approach him for help. Much more about him surfaced during our meetings. During our first meeting over lunch, I learned enough about Sean to know that he was a switch flipper and that he was someone that I wanted to interview.

Sean was twenty-two years of age and a native Oregonian. He was born in Portland, which had been his home except for a short time spent in California. His parents divorced when he was in the seventh grade. Sean currently lived with his mother, except when he was in Eugene pursuing his college education at the University of Oregon. When we first agreed that he would be interviewed, he clearly stated that he would be "putting everything on the table." His personal transparency was everything he said it would be.

A "roller coaster experience" was how Sean described the last four years of his life. Sean struggled with mental illness and all the diagnoses that came with it. Doctors had been trying to figure it out for quite some time. In the sixth grade, he was tested for attention deficit disorder. Sean stated that during early school years, it was very hard for him to sit at a desk and go through multiple pages of schoolwork. He always felt compelled to be up and moving. The test for ADD concluded that he had an atypical form of the disorder. While it didn't resolve the problem, it helped somewhat that he attended a private school where the student-to-staff ratio was six to one.

While a student at Claremont College in California, Sean had a complete psychotic break. Sean described what had happened to him and how he'd felt. His life was a tortured existence during that time. He described being on a manic high for extremely long periods of time, feeling enormously creative and energetic; entertaining concepts came out of his mind and amazed him. His psychotic break became severe enough that he had to be hospitalized. Coming down from the high was painful. He didn't really want to come down. It was a rarified atmosphere to be in the so-called manic state. From 2009 to 2010, Sean was treated with medications and other mental health resources. He told me that his condition made him feel very odd.

"It was like I was in a dream state that lasted for months. Sometimes I couldn't tell if I was in a dream or in reality," he explained.

Following that extremely difficult time, Sean began the process of flipping some switches. He emphasized, "I had to relearn literally everything and piece back together what reality was to me." A lot was packed into that sentence. Sean described his condition during that time as an atrophy of his mental abilities.

"It was like I had to use a walker for my brain." He went through a challenging time of retraining his brain. Please understand that neither Sean nor I are contending that one can just decide to flip a switch and cure mental illness. The flipping of the switch for Sean involved using his willpower and intelligence, in addition to external resources, to work on his illness. Retraining his brain involved a lot of willpower and self-discipline. Having missed so much of his college work, it became necessary for Sean to leave Claremont College and live closer to family in the Portland area.

Sean is an amazing person with an amazing attitude. It is indicative of his attitude when he says, "I'm grateful for the experience and for the state of mind that I went through. It has made me realize the great potential of the human mind." That attitude is a huge indication of his ability to do reflective thinking rather than reactive thinking. Sean likes the phrase "The mind is like a parachute; it only works when it's open."

Meditation is a valuable tool for Sean. It puts him in a relaxed state in which he can explore concepts in a controlled manner. Controlling his thought processes and his thought content has been another valuable asset for him. He contends that, for him, it is a form of flipping the switch. It is *his* decision what thoughts and concepts he will allow his mind to explore. That has been very important to Sean in creating, stabilizing, and securing his identity. Sean contends that it is important for everyone to identify what his own reality is at the present—but then, not simply try to justify that present reality, but flip the switch from the present and pursue the new identity one desires for himself.

Part of Sean's thinking involves the idea that human life is made up of habits. He believes that in many ways, humans are on autopilot. Influential in his thinking are concepts such as the "OK Plateau" in the book *Moonwalking with Einstein* by Joshua Foer. Sean summarizes the concept with the statement that many people convince themselves that they are okay with who they are and acquiesce in staying there. They have reached a plateau. Flipping the switch, he further contends, is breaking habits and not getting stuck in an undesirable state. Further, individuals remold their identity by examining those habits that hold them back—both habitual actions and habitual thoughts, and acting on the ones that need action.

Through his struggles and successes, Sean has embraced the idea that being honest with oneself is essential to both physical and mental health. But one must remember to also be realistic.

"Flipping the switch can be in small steps that are right in front of you," he says. "It can be a mistake to try to jump from where you are to where you want to be without realizing there may be many steps between the two. As Gandhi said, 'Your beliefs become your thoughts, your thoughts become your words. Your words become your actions, your actions become your habits. Your habits become your values, your values become your destiny.'"

Sean is correct when he contends that there are an infinite number of switches. It is up to individuals to choose the switches appropriate for them, place their hands on those switches, and flip them. Sean calls this "cultivating intentionality." It's a great concept. The individual moves forward by consciously cultivating and acting on those things they intend to do, become, realize, act upon, and imagine.

I am very impressed by how much this man has learned in his twenty-two years and how much wisdom accompanies it. Much of that has been born out of his struggles. At the same time, I am impressed by the fact that his illness does not contain or define him. He is an upbeat, energetic, spiritual, warm person. He has much to offer the world and perhaps especially those who struggle in similar ways.

Sean is looking forward, evidenced by his enrollment at the University of Oregon. He is pursuing a degree in marketing and packaging design. Being an open-minded thinker and a talented artist will go a long way in helping him achieve his new identity. Examples of his art may be viewed at www.ludemanart.com.

■ ■ ■

It is amazing how a personal perspective transformation can happen at unexpected moments and in unexpected places. One morning, on my way to my office, I stopped by the mall to make a purchase. I was in a hurry to get in, get out, and be on my way. As I walked through the mall, I noticed a small group of young men gathered around a framed object. I was curious enough to ease toward them to see what it was they were studying so intensely.

As I got closer, I began to notice that the five guys were dressed in clothing that was, shall we say, very different from what I was wearing. There were the baggy jeans that were in danger of falling to their knees. How do they keep those from actually falling down? There were hats turned sideways, tattoos, wild hairstyles, and just generally not the kind of attire I was used to seeing. I have to admit that my mind gravitated toward thoughts such as "They must be gang members."

I eased up behind them so as not to disturb whatever they were doing and quietly looked over their shoulders. What I saw was a framed picture that was digitized in such a way that the picture was not viewable. But if someone gazed at it for a while and in a slightly cross-eyed manner, one was supposed to see the picture.

I did that. Gazed, crossed my eyes, tilted my head, moved my head a little back and a little forward. The guys may have had odd thoughts about me too! Still, I couldn't make out the picture. I finally got up the nerve to ask one of the guys what I was supposed to see in the picture.

"It's a picture of God," he informed me. "Can *you* see God in the picture?"

I had to admit that I could not see God nor anyone else in the picture no matter how I contorted my head and eyes. To my astonishment, he said, "Well, it's better to know God than to see Him."

Wow! I was completely astonished by his reply. The transformation of my perspective concerning him and his friends was totally amazing! That young man will never know what an influence he had on my mind that day. I got slapped in the face by my own assumptions and by a faulty perspective. I knew that it was totally wrong to assume anything by the way a person was dressed. But that moment, that perspective transformation for that particular situation, is one that I will always remember.

William James, a Harvard psychologist, claimed that a great discovery for his generation was that "changed attitudes usually precede changed lives." I agree that it is a choice each person is given. How we respond to situations by our attitudes on a daily basis has a tremendous impact on our lives.

James is correct, yet I would take his assertion one step back. Experience tells us that often a perspective transformation must happen before there can be an attitude change. The power of perspective is huge in just about any issue in life. When a perspective is transformed, it is changed. For example, take cigarette smoking. Some people smoke and feel that it is their right to do so. Certainly, without endangering others, it *is* their right. Those people look at continuing to smoke from the perspective of their rights. However, when those same individuals have a serious examination of the issue of smoking with their doctor, and the results are shown clearly on x-rays of either themselves or others, their minds begin to change. They transform from a perspective of *rights* to a perspective oriented around the *outcomes* of cancer, emphysema, stroke, disability, loss of control, death, and more. The outcomes become central to themselves and to people around them.

Simply saying "I'm going to have a positive attitude today" won't last very long. A transformed or changed perspective precedes a changed attitude, which precedes a changed life. You can change your attitude and change your life, but often a changed perspective is required before the attitudinal and life changes can happen.

Once the attitude changes through a perspective transformation, it can have a tremendous impact on

- the way the day proceeds from there;
- relationships with others who may receive the benefits or the fallout;

- emotional health for hours and days to come;
- creative and performance issues; or
- your sense of centeredness.

A good attitude doesn't mean rolling over and accepting whatever comes down the pike. It isn't a "Pollyanna" approach or a sense of denial that something happening to you is wrong, difficult, or unjust. You have the right to stand up for yourself or someone else, and not let circumstances take control over you and advantage of you. It is *how* you stand up for yourself that makes the difference. When acted against, it is often a default reaction to retaliate. And those retaliations are not always short-lived but can be acted out over many years or even a lifetime. In the short term, it can be a knee-jerk reaction. What did you feel like doing the last time a vehicle cut you off yet the driver gave *you* the single-digit salute?

I was approaching an interstate on-ramp in Indianapolis. The traffic going onto the ramp was not supposed to stop, but the cross-street traffic had stop signs. As I approached the intersection, I noticed a car start up from one of the stop signs and move into the intersection. It was necessary for me to hit my brakes hard to avoid hitting the other car. The driver also hit her brakes and came to a halt, looking at me from the driver's side of her car.

I assumed she'd realized her mistake and would be embarrassed about it. So I smiled at her and waited for her to move on and clear my path onto the interstate. I was slightly shocked when she gave me a vulgar gesture with both hands. That was accompanied by some well-articulated words of unpleasant greeting. As she moved on with her car, her two little children had picked up the language and attitude and were making it known from the back window. Then I noticed something that made me laugh out loud. It was a bumper sticker that read, "There are no problems that God and I can't handle!"

Life is full of contradictions in others, in you, and in me. A productive attitude can erode in an instant. But it doesn't have to continue. Anger is a normal emotion. But what you do with it impacts you more than anyone else.

I was attending a convention on the East Coast when I received a phone call from my physician. I stepped out to take the call and heard him say, "Your test results have been returned to me. Wayne, the results cannot rule out cancer. You need to have a biopsy as soon as it's convenient."

"Should I fly home immediately to have that done?" I asked with more calm than I felt.

"No, finish your work there, and I'll schedule it in a couple of weeks."

I talked with him a bit further, ended the conversation, and turned off my cell phone. I needed to think. "Wham! I didn't see that coming! Cancer? Biopsy? This isn't really happening, is it? This is really getting serious!"

I immediately told my wife and tried to sound low-key about it. I wasn't fooling her. She was very supportive and vowed we would just take the situation one step at a time—together.

Three weeks later, I received the biopsy results while in my office. Yes, I did have cancer. My hopes for negative test results were dashed. Our little seven-year-old granddaughter, along with her mom, dad, and my wife, had come to my office for a family trip to the zoo. I never told our granddaughter about the cancer but chose my words carefully so that my family would know what was going on without alarming the child. On the trip to the zoo, Madysen had been very quiet. But she proved just how perceptive children could be when she suddenly said, "I don't want you to die!" I was stunned that she perceived the seriousness of something that had not been told to her. I gave her a hug and a kiss and assured her that I would do my very best to honor her request!

Being and doing are twin parts of attitude that have an impact on yourself and those around you. One is the state in which you find yourself and the acknowledgment of that state. The other is a pathway to do something about that state of being. How I reacted to cancer during those trying times made a big difference in my health and even my pain level.

The situation was real. I couldn't escape the reality of it even though at times I felt desperate to wake up and find that it was all a bad dream. Surgery, pain, and uncertainty were going to be part of my life for a while. My state of being as a cancer patient was a certainty. One of the troubling aspects was the realization that there was no way to avoid it. There was only one way out, and that was through the middle of it all. Though I never found myself in the "I can't" mode of thinking, I had to move from "if I can't" beat this cancer and its ramifications to "if I can" beat this cancer and eventually to "I can" beat this cancer.

So that was my state of *being* and the reality of my life. The other side of the coin was *doing*. I realized that even though the only way out was through, I had some choices in how I would react and what I would do about it. Yes, I had to do something about the treatment choices, follow-up options, and other things to consider. But just as important was what I was going to do about my emotional and spiritual attitudes and reactions.

I could have crawled into an emotional hole as a result of reactive thinking. But instead, I became reflective about my present and future. I was a cancer patient, but I was not a cancer person. My cancer, as with college failure, was not going to define me. There were things I could do about it. One choice was to become emotionally immobilized by fear. Another choice was to be resentful and angry that my family and I were being forced to go through such a mortality reality check. None of those choices were acceptable. With the help of my wonderful wife, daughter, son, and family, I came to the attitude that there were rewards in the midst of almost everything in life—even cancer.

Finally, what I did about my fear was admit it, accept it, and find ways to deal with it. Doing that was tough, but it helped me gain more of a sense of control in my life. I read literature that fed me spiritually and emotionally. My wife and I love humor, so we watched funny sitcoms. She made sure I ate a healthy diet that included plenty of antioxidants. I was fortunate to have our daughter and son living in Portland. Sometimes just having people you love with you touches the soul more than words.

Let me make this clear, I never want to have cancer again! I'm healed, cured, and healthy. But in the midst of pain and uncertainty were times of delicious blessings:

- I became closer to my family. We've always been close, but during that time we became closer. I knew that vulnerability can cause some people with life-threatening illnesses to reach out with openness, or it may cause them to retreat into emotional isolation, which folds back onto itself.
- I grew spiritually. My prayer life increased as did my reading of material that fed me. My wife and I often read the same material, and it was amazing how similar our insights were.
- My sense of awareness became more pronounced. I noticed so much more in life around me. I found humor in things that I probably would have missed earlier.
- Forgiveness became easier. On the morning of my surgery, while in the little holding room, I was thinking that I just wanted this to be over and have nothing go wrong. About that time, a distinguished-looking man pulled back the curtain, walked in, and sat next to my bed. "I'm Doctor Smith," he said. "I'm going to be doing your hernia repair." With a sinking feeling, I blurted, "Oh, you mean I have a hernia in *addition* to cancer?" The poor man blanched, looked at my wristband, and backed out of the room with sincere apologies. In an amazing twist, there were two William Wayne Browns being

operated on that morning! I was a little unnerved but found it very funny. Maybe it was "two-for-one Monday."

- My sincere and sensitive appreciation for each kindness and word of encouragement became deeply sharpened.
- I learned to put fewer limits on myself. If I wanted to go somewhere, I went. If I wanted to take a nap, I took one. If I wanted to take my wife out for breakfast, I took her. I was kinder to myself and less driven when I didn't feel like being driven.
- Petty things showed themselves unworthy of any of my life moments. Life moments for me became amazingly sweeter and richer. Honestly, I have to remind myself of that many times. Life moves forward, and old patterns of thinking can creep back into both our being and our doing.

Flipping the switch is part of the challenge during serious illness. I share that part of my journey to show you that, even during the dark times, there is the opportunity to make choices that move you from a state of being to a state of doing. Acknowledgment of the first is necessary, but the rewards of the second are greater.

Illness is not always diagnosed as something that can be excised. Often, it isn't even recognized by the person suffering from it. Just as importantly, many people don't recognize the connection of their history with their present situation.

■ ■ ■

Anita's Story

Anita's story is about a journey from being reared by immature parents, through some difficult and dark times, and emerging later in life as a woman at peace.

That long journey began in Salem, Oregon, where she was born to well-meaning but egocentric parents. Their behavior included their attitudes toward their children. As Anita puts it, "Kids didn't count for much. Parents were the most important." She contends that her parents were not physically abusive. Mostly, they neglected her and her siblings. They lived in a huge house with her cousins, aunts, and uncles. Lots of people took care of them until sometime after age two.

Anita's dad came home from war, which caused more difficulty in relationships than joy. Her mom and dad didn't get along, so Anita and her siblings went to live with a grandmother, and then alternated back and forth between the grandmother and her parents. By about age nine, she moved in with her grandparents on a permanent basis. She describes the years with her grandparents as wonderful.

"They loved us unconditionally," she states with a light in her eyes. Her grandparents gave the children a strong faith. The years with them nurturing her stood in stark contrast to what she'd received from her parents.

Anita knows now that her mom was emotionally immature and didn't know how to raise children, because she herself hadn't received much rearing. The same was true for her dad. Anita's mom hated her dad, because she saw him as a womanizer. In spite of his faults, Anita loved her dad, describing him as being kind and good to her as opposed to her mother, who was insulting and demeaning.

During third grade, a court ruled that her father was to have full custody. Anita did well in school during that time and liked her teacher. But then, her father married his pregnant girlfriend. The living situation deteriorated severely for Anita and for her siblings with a new stepmother in the house. Using the new situation as leverage, Anita's mom went to court and regained custody.

Anita's dad had also become a member of a religion where it was customary to take children door-to-door as a method of gaining access to the homes. She greatly resented being used that way. Ironically, Anita felt that God had forsaken her.

Anita's grandfather eventually became her sole source of comfort, as well as the epitome of what a male role model should be. But he lived far away, and she only got to see him on occasional weekends. Later, Anita came to a fuller understanding of what it meant to have a healthy expression of one's faith.

Her mother later remarried, and Anita moved back in with them. Her mom wanted the kids back, and it became a time of stability and security for Anita and her siblings. That was mainly due to her stepfather. Anita liked him very much. She describes her stepfather as a godsend for her and her brother's life. She still sees her stepfather and enjoys him tremendously.

Anita grew up and attended college. She dated a young man who was Catholic, and she eventually joined his church. They married and had children. Tragically, her husband drowned. During that time, she found her faith, a sense of reverence, and a sense of safety.

Anita and her second husband, Jerry, met at a department store where they were both employed. With a twinkle in her eyes, she relates that the two of them began to see each other with new perspectives at a Christmas party sponsored by the store. They had fun, laughed a lot, and felt comfortable and at ease with each other. It was significant that she loved his parents. They decided to get married and have now been together for more than forty-five years. During those years, Anita and Jerry had a lot of fun skiing, playing tennis, and golfing. But during those years, drinking also became a problem.

Anita thought alcohol helped her to be herself and lowered her inhibitions. It became a part of their lifestyle. Their children began experimenting with marijuana and other drugs during their teen years. As a sophomore in high school, their son asked to be locked up to help him stay away from drugs. Anita remembers that he was a hopeless addict. They put him in a drug rehabilitation center for thirty days. During that time, she discovered and fully owned that she was an alcoholic. In a brave move, she got rid of all alcohol in their home and in her life. But her craving for alcohol remained so strong that she was tempted to break her promise to her husband and son.

Anita describes her first Alcoholics Anonymous meeting as very emotional, and it remained that way for six months. "I didn't talk. I just cried," she recalls. Finally, she flipped the switch, stood up, and said, "I'm Anita. I'm an alcoholic." Astonishingly, her cravings went away! Anita asserts that she was wrong about God having forsaken her all those years.

Anita had been a massage therapist. But in 2001, she closed her office. Presently, she and her husband have a very solid marriage. They have been through the fire and have been galvanized by adversity. Their son found great help in rehabilitation services, and he is now employed and a contributing member of society.

To meet and speak with Anita, one would never guess the challenges she faced in life. But she flipped the switch and continues to flip it each day. As for the future, Anita says that she is taking it day by day.

"Each day I open the book of my life and let it play out."

What a captivating way to look at daily life!

Making It Personal

1. **What attitudes in your life could use a perspective transformation?** (Examples: negativity, fear, complacency, racism, etc.)
2. **How are they impacting your flipping the switch toward a more fulfilling life?** (Examples: missing out on relationships, lack of initiative, closing doors for yourself, etc.)
3. **How can you put yourself onto the pathway of transforming your perspective on those issues?** (Examples: reading, studying, discussion, interaction with uncomfortable situations, etc.)

CHAPTER 11
If You're Not Yet a Diamond, At Least Be Semiprecious

The difference between a lump of coal and a diamond is time and pressure. No one wants to be thought of as a lump of coal, nor should anyone think of himself or herself that way. Metaphorically speaking, if you're not yet a diamond, you can at least function as a smoky topaz on your way to the diamond state.

Still, most of us have not reached the diamond stage either. And that's fine! Somewhere between the two ways of thinking about oneself is a healthy self-perspective. Realizing that we're somewhere between that lump of coal and a diamond opens exciting and real possibilities for development, both now and in the future.

Being a diamond is just a symbol for a life that is significant in the mind of the one who is living it. I can't define what a diamond life is for someone else. Neither can you. Looking toward being a diamond doesn't mean that the present has no thrill. Many people describe their lives as a journey; the trip is just as fulfilling as the destination. And doesn't the destination often move as we get closer to it? One of the ideas that I emphasize to many people who are flipping their switch is that the process of moving forward can be very rewarding. The expectation and anticipation of the future is often just as exciting as the realization of it.

I have heard people say, "You can be anything you want to be!" Actually, that is probably not true. Not everyone can be president of the United States. It's just not realistic. For one thing, most people don't have enough money! Not everyone can be everything. *However, you can be enormously more than what you cannot be.* A huge gift to yourself is to do the homework earlier in this book relative to finding out who you are, your aptitudes, your interests—especially those things for which you have a sense of passion. And remember that your passion does not necessarily have to be what you do for a living.

Here are some things to keep in mind as you move through time and pressure toward being a diamond. *Avoid cockiness and arrogance.* I have observed a strange phenomenon among some people who have not flipped the switch from inertia toward action. Some have a cocky, arrogant attitude that is never warranted. In my opinion, cockiness is never acceptable, especially in people who really do need to flip that switch and get real. Remember, no one wants to hear you talk about how great you are at, well, anything.

A cocky and arrogant attitude has several things wrong with it. It usually precedes a humbling moment. Life has enough ability to take you down a notch without you adding to it. An arrogant attitude is equivalent to a "kick me" sign attached to your posterior. It telegraphs shallowness and lack of substance. And it is a people repellant. A cocky, arrogant attitude repels most people, rather than attracting them and the opportunities they may bring. Remember, the nectar of adulation is best consumed with humility.

The answer? *Get real confidence.* Instead of a cocky, arrogant attitude, get some real confidence. The difference between arrogance and confidence is reality. It is the realization that your gifts, abilities, and accomplishments are real, not imaginary.

Gaining appropriate confidence in yourself can greatly strengthen your resolve and ability to flip the switch. Otherwise, you are flat-footed and deflated. As you move toward the "I can" thinking mode, identify one area in which you would like to have more confidence. For example, would an improvement in managing your finances give you more confidence? If so, take steps to move from seeing yourself as a lump of coal *in that aspect* of your life.

You may want to check on that 401(k) and know exactly what is happening. Don't know what's happening in your IRA account? Check on it. Yes, maybe it has gone down, but then maybe it has gone up in value. Your contributions to the account may be buying you more shares during a downturn in their value. If the value has gone down, maybe you need to get some professional advice on rearranging your investments to stem the downward trend. Getting the facts helps you control the fear in your life. Most people like to know their true situation rather than being blackmailed by the unknown. Not knowing bullies you with fear! Don't let it. As you become informed, that information helps you claim a feeling of confidence because you have more sense of control.

Now, check yourself in the mirror. Without getting narcissistic, look at yourself with an eye toward the image you are projecting. As you prepare to flip the switch from inertia toward accomplishing life goals, from being stuck in "I can't" and moving toward "I can," the image you project to others is important. Our culture has adopted a dress and appearance code that sometimes gives people the wrong impression. In other words, personal appearance does matter. Yes, character, ability, and integrity matter more, but they don't have to be exclusive of personal appearance. Rarely does anyone have a second chance to make a first impression.

When I was looking for an executive assistant, I advertised the position in several venues, one of which was the "help wanted" section in the newspaper. The personal appearance of the people who applied, both male and female, ran the gamut from a very positive first impression to those who even touched a sense of anger in me at the disrespect they displayed. My executive assistant would often be my representative at functions where I could not be present. It was important that he or she projected a professional, pleasant, and approachable impression. So remember, your appearance may be important to your boss for the same reason—you are representing him or her.

I staunchly advocate that everyone is entitled to his or her own style of dress and personal appearance. However, if you want to project an image of confidence in a professional situation as you move toward flipping the switch, you are going to have to consider what others believe about you by what you show them. Can appearances be deceiving? Remember my mall incident? Absolutely they can be deceiving, but they *are* what is presented first. Remember, present yourself appropriately for the occasion. I'm confident that those young men in the mall would not dress that way if they were applying for a job that required a more tailored image.

As I've said before, the most deceitful results happen upon looking into a mirror alone. Another way of checking yourself in the mirror is to ask your boss or supervisor for a performance review. But first allow him or her time to make a quick trip to the coronary unit before coming back to ask you, "What!" Rarely does a person in authority have someone ask for a performance review. If you trust your employer to be honest and upfront with you, a voluntary performance review can be an invaluable tool to you, and perhaps a respect enhancer for your boss.

For one thing, you will learn how you are viewed in terms of your work performance. You won't have to wonder anymore if you are perceived negatively in some areas, on par with everyone else, or excelling in other aspects of your work. Yes, it's a bit risky, but again, I would rather know than wonder. Also, knowing how you are perceived gives you a chance to ameliorate those areas where you believe you may have been incorrectly perceived. But be prepared to back up those corrections with facts. Finally, a voluntary performance review becomes part of your file. If you ask for a raise, you have something on which to base your request. If you are downgraded in areas not mentioned in the review, you have an inconsistency that can be honestly and fairly pointed out.

If part of your switch flipping involves asserting "*I can have better interpersonal communication with my family and friends,*" then make sure you *check your attitude.* That is, how are you coming across to others with your speech and mannerisms?

Most basic communication classes offer to record a video of you reading a story or, better yet, telling a story. You can even do this at home. Simply set up your camcorder, smartphone, or other video device. Then, either standing or sitting in front of it, give a three-to-five minute narrative about yourself—where you were born, where you live now, your work, your family, etc. Another exercise could involve relating an incident that happened in your life. But make sure you organize your thoughts. The old saying is true: more baled hay will fit on a wagon than what is simply thrown onto it.

Next, play back the recording and watch yourself. Uncomfortable already? Most people are uncomfortable watching themselves on a recording. But it is very valuable. Avoid the mistake of being overly critical or overly affirming of yourself. Examine the quality and inflection of your voice, your eye contact, posture, nonverbal communication, such as gestures, and the overall effectiveness of the presentation.

Ask yourself, "If I saw this video as a potential employer, significant other, friend, or during a first-time encounter with someone, would I be turned off by me?"

After you have viewed it, ask an impartial person to view it and give you his or her impressions. This is where a life coach can be very helpful. She will give you her impressions of your communication skills without an axe to grind. The attitude you display is a huge part of your communication with others. It can make people want to hear and see more, or it can make them feel like sixty seconds is an hour.

Now, I'm not advocating that you be a fake. Instead, if you know where you want to go with your life after you have flipped the switch from inertia to action, then *act accordingly!* Want to be a musician in a band? Then *think* like a musician in a band, and surround yourself with that culture. Want to become better at language skills? Then *think* like a linguist, and surround yourself with those tools and practice using them. Thinking it won't make it true without actually flipping the switch. But it will put your mind in the position to recognize steps and opportunities toward the actuality of your desires. Move yourself from wishing to being.

Visualization is a big help here. Get into the habit of visualizing yourself flipping the switch, moving into "I can" thinking, and then doing what your heart desires. I found visualization very helpful during my cancer battle, as I visualized my cancer cells being destroyed by the antioxidants in my body. While not relying on visualization as my only approach to overcoming cancer, it is very possible that such visualization helped boost the immune system.

Most people are familiar with the concept of dressing for the way they want to become. If you want to flip the switch toward achieving a new image that projects confidence, you will need to believe in yourself enough to start acting confident. Some basketball coaches train their players to visually see the ball going into the net before they shoot, during the shot, and even *after* the shot. Between practices they are told to constantly visualize each aspect of their shooting maneuver—getting set, posturing, releasing the ball, following through, and watching the ball enter the hoop with nothing but net.

In a large measure, you are what you think you are. If your mind is filled with "I can't" images that you either give yourself or that you allow others to give you, then that is what your body and actions will reveal to others. Once you determine that you will flip the switch, your position is "*I can* become more confident." Then you will be on your road to *being* more confident. Let me tell you about someone who is on her way to being a diamond, but is also happy in the state of being she is currently in.

■ ■ ■

Tanya Hawkins's Story

Tanya Hawkins has a heart for the homeless. But her journey to arrive there was circuitous, to say the least. Tanya was born in Rockford, Illinois, where her single mother reared her and two younger siblings. Her mother worked long hours, and Tanya was left alone to take care of the other children.

Her mom was fifteen years of age when Tanya was born. It struck me that the whole family—mother and three children—were *all* children. Her mom kicked Tanya out of the home when Tanya turned sixteen. She moved in with her boyfriend and was able to secure a job at a department store and even became manager.

At eighteen, she moved to Peru, Illinois, and met a twenty-nine-year-old man who enticed her into drugs. After overdosing twice, she lost her job and subsequently lost everything else. Additionally, the man soon lost his business and his employees. All due to drug abuse.

They moved to Portland, Oregon, and found an apartment. Tanya tells me that she prayed a lot. She eventually got a job at a temporary service agency. It was about this time that Tanya realized she needed to get away from drugs. The temp agency placed her at an upscale apartment complex as a receptionist. A customer was so impressed with her that he wanted to hire her for his business. She passed the drug test for employment and was hired. Wisely, Tanya decided to leave her boyfriend and the influence of drugs.

These actions gave Tanya a different perspective on the negative influence of her boyfriend on her life and the devastating influence of drugs on her health and her sanity. She had a perspective transformation. As a result, she quit drugs cold turkey! That was a huge flip of the switch that could not have been possible, she contends, without an astounding amount of self-realization.

Tanya moved into a studio apartment that was offered by her new employer. She still had a lot of debt, but her self-determination led her to become the top leasing consultant. Thanks to her stellar performance, the owner of the apartment complex moved her to each new building site over a five-year period. Incredibly, her employer chose her to be the regional trainer for his other leasing agents.

In 2001, Tanya married a resident named Ben who was also a coworker. She went to church with her new husband and thoroughly enjoyed the experience. Tanya says, "The pastor's sermons were so good that I actually thought he was talking to me! It really spoke to me." Although their marriage ended after only six months, Ben had introduced her to her faith.

Tanya says that another switch flipped for her when 9/11 happened. She felt the world was ending and, seeking comfort and direction, returned to church. She met a man there and moved in with him. However, she couldn't shake the feeling that what she was doing was wrong, so she moved out. Through it all, her former husband, Ben, was still there for her. She became convinced that God was telling her that Ben was the man with whom she was to spend the rest of her life. He proposed again, and they remarried. They have now been married for many years.

Soon after, her employers sold the apartment complexes to another company, and Tanya found herself unemployed and forced to work various odd jobs. Not long after that, Tanya had a miscarriage and experienced other emotional and physical problems, including anxiety attacks. On top of that, her grandmother died from cancer, compounding the stressors in Tanya's life.

But again, Tanya flipped a switch. Not wanting to watch another significant person in her life die due to poor lifestyle, she began to take charge of her life. She began carefully managing her finances and went from a low credit score to an eight hundred!

After leaving property management, Tanya began working escrow accounts. But once again, she lost her job due to the collapse of the housing market. For a brief time, she tried selling high-end vacuum cleaners. Around that time, a girlfriend asked her to help with a coffee cart that she was running for the homeless. It was a service through which pastries, coffee, and sandwiches were distributed to homeless people on the streets of Portland. It was a very touching experience for Tanya, and over the next few months, she even handed out some of her husband's socks! She and her friend held garage sales with the proceeds helping to fund the coffee cart program.

As a result of her experiences with the coffee cart, Tanya founded Gung Ho Ministries while continuing to do the coffee cart twice each month. Tanya then opened a not-for-profit resale shop to help fund Gung Ho Ministries. The shop receives donations of good clothing and household items that are then sold in the store. The profits help the coffee cart but also veterans' families with issues such as transitional housing, assistance with the purchase of a home, and other needs.

Tanya is extremely energetic and outgoing, which is a big help in her fund-raising efforts as well as her interpersonal relationships. She owes so much of her personal and emotional success to flipping the switch in her life at various points. Tanya wants to get out of debt so that she can expand Gung Ho Ministries.

"I have a heart for the homeless," she says, "because I was almost that way myself."

Today, Tanya is quickly becoming a multifaceted gem!

Making It Personal

1. **Identify and write down what you see as your diamond points.** In other words, what are the aspects of your life that help you sparkle and shine? (Examples: openness, good listener, analytical thinking, organization, compassion, etc.)
2. **Where are the lumps of coal in your life?** (Examples: personality problems, addiction, attitude, procrastination, etc.)
3. **How will you begin using your diamond points to help you move forward?** How will you begin developing your lumps of coal into beneficial aspects of your life—or at least, keep them from holding you back?

CHAPTER 12
Tripping Points & Tipping Points

Tripping points are the ways in which individuals interact with life through the filters of their very personal, and often guarded, outlook on life. Tripping points are the aspects and events of life that can create obstacles on the pathway. They may even cause some individuals to fail at moving forward.

Tripping points can include a wide variety of issues. Below are eight areas that I have observed to be factors contributing to individuals tripping on their way to flipping their personal switches. They include

- self-consciousness about either our inabilities or abilities (maybe both);
- cherished, ingrained biases;
- unproductive personality segments;
- the way we deal with people;

- views of conflict;
- how we were reared;
- our relationships with family members, including parents and siblings; and
- a lack of thankfulness and appreciation.

1. **Self-consciousness about abilities and inabilities.** This is a two-faced problem. Some people have a negative view of their own abilities. Certainly you have experienced people who you know are talented and have much potential, but who cannot be convinced of their abilities. They are stuck in the "I can't" stage of personal development. And yet they secretly wish they could do more and achieve more.

   At the same time, there are those who think they have more abilities than they really possess. These people may be perceived as arrogant and unapproachable, at least upon first meeting them. Maybe they've never heard the saying "You can catch more flies with honey than with vinegar."

   If you belong in either of these categories, it is best to let someone else help you come to a realistic appraisal of your abilities. Want to play golf but don't think you are good enough? Get a golf coach. You already play golf but think you are really great? Get a golf coach!

2. **Cherished, ingrained biases.** "An unfair preference or dislike of something" is one of the definitions given for *bias* by the *Encarta World English Dictionary*.

There is nothing wrong with preferring chocolate ice cream above all other flavors. However, if I make judgments about people based on their preference for black-cherry ice cream, then it becomes an unfair bias. It is unfair because the choice of ice cream should have nothing to do with judging another person's intrinsic value.

That's a very simple example. However, it is astounding how some people make judgments about situations and people on evidence almost as shallow as ice cream preference—judgments that can blind them to opportunities for flipping the switch. According to *Encarta*, a bias can also be "a line that runs diagonally across the weave of a fabric." Imagine how many biases run against the fabric of life!

3. **Unproductive personality segments.** I call this tripping point "personality segments" instead of personality traits. The reason is to emphasize that segments of an individual's personality can very easily influence other segments of that same personality. For example, if someone has a segment of his personality that is demeaning to others, such as friends or even casual acquaintances, it will likely carry over to the segment of his personality that relates to his ability to make friends. It will likely carry over to the segment of his personality that relates to family relationships. These are just two examples out of perhaps dozens of other segments that could possibly be influenced.

I was shopping with my wife in a large discount store and was lingering near the checkout lines waiting for her. Suddenly, I was astounded to observe a very ugly man accompanied by his wife. The ugliness to which I'm referring is not a physical ugliness but a *personality* ugliness. The poor woman was simply trying to make up her mind whether to purchase an item or leave it. While she deliberated, he very loudly yelled, "Make up your goddamn mind, or else I'm going to leave!" He went on cursing and grousing so much that people were beginning to stare. I kept thinking how much better off she would have been if he had actually left! Concerned that whatever I might say would exacerbate the situation, I stayed close at hand in case the situation became physical.

An examination of your personality is well worth the time. By doing so, it's possible that unproductive aspects can be uncovered, examined, and improved upon so that the switch can be flipped toward more or improved productivity.

4. **The way we deal with people.** The way one person deals with another person relates to how he or she views fairness and honesty. Unless someone is amoral or a sociopath, he or she is bound to have some level of sensitivity when dealing with other human beings. To move from any of the "I can't" levels to "I can" requires a healthy examination of how one deals with, or gives significance to, other people.

Understandably, the level of significance given to anyone can depend on the relationship between the two people. The level of significance I give to my family is very different from the significance I give to a random motorist on the highway. If an individual is dealing with an "I can't/if I can't/if I can" situation, it is healthy to examine what significance is being placed on those who are players in the scenario. The significance you give may be the significance you receive.

I was driving home late one night, lost in thought after a busy day of conflict mediation. I confess that I was a little bit worried about the conflict situation, and it probably showed on my face. As I stopped for a traffic light, another car drove up beside me in the left lane. The four teenagers in the car were glancing over at me. I smiled at them and then politely looked forward again. A tap on the horn of the other car brought my attention to the left again. To my astonishment, they weren't being rude. Instead, the two girls *and* the two boys blew me a kiss, gave me the thumbs-up, smiled, and nodded at me. What I got was, "You're okay; we just want to send you a kind message." I was touched beyond expression!

At the beginning of the encounter, the significance I attached to the other car's occupants was neutral and emotionally noncommittal. *After* the brief encounter and the actions they displayed, the significance I attached to them was greatly changed

to the point that I will probably always remember them.
5. **Views of conflict.** Far be it for me to condense here libraries of material on conflict management and resolution. I have had more training in that subject than I ever intended, but I have to admit that it has come in handy in my life and work. How a person views and responds to conflict can greatly influence his or her process of flipping the switch from inertia to forward movement.

Conflict affects everyone: conflict at work, conflict in family relationships, conflict between neighbors, and so forth. To live is to become involved in conflict of some sort at various times in life. Have you considered that conflict is not always with others? You may even have conflict with yourself: conflicting emotions, conflicting ambitions, conflicting thoughts, even conflicting self-image.

In dealing with conflict, consider all views, internal and external. In dealing with conflict management with individuals and groups, one of the hardest hurdles is getting people to stop making an Olympic sport out of jumping to conclusions.

Yes, conflict can be a positive thing if it is handled well and if it eventually improves the relationships of those involved. But for conflict to be the most productive, it must have all parties willing to seek a solution rather than a way to hurt each other. The kind of conflict that either openly or insidiously causes damage to the other person rarely, if ever, raises the level of humanity and sanity of those involved.

If the conflict resolution efforts are ineffective, consider having someone mediate between the parties. If the other parties are unwilling to work with a mediator, seek help for yourself so that you can find stability and some measure of peace. Those who seek to harm others by being unkind, unfair, and untruthful ultimately hurt themselves. Don't fall into that trap.

6. **How we were reared.** When I was writing my dissertation at Indiana University, I referred to myself as having been "raised in a small-town environment." My dissertation chairperson asserted that people are reared and vegetables are raised.

Whether you honor that distinction or not, you will notice that the context of this book, including the interviews I share with you, takes into account how the individuals have been reared. Earlier in this writing, I encouraged you to seriously consider your personal journey and to write down where you have been in your life.

Include in that reflection the way you were brought up. You were not brought to this point in your life to be a vegetable. You are a human being with a history, a present, and a future. The values you have in life, your views of humankind, your outlook on work, your view of yourself, and many other values have been placed in your mind at least partially by the influences on you from birth until now. They are a part of the fabric of your life.

Some people very much affirm the way they were reared. Some completely rebel against their earlier rearing. And some examine their rearing, affirm the best parts, and release the unappealing parts. Be very aware that in flipping the switch from one aspect of your life toward what you choose as more positive, you must consider the influences of your rearing.

7. **Thankfulness.**

    As we express our gratitude, we must never forget that the highest appreciation is not to utter words, but to live by them.

    —John F. Kennedy

    Having a grateful attitude is a wonderful tipping point. I have to wonder at people who have an entitlement attitude, or rather, people who aren't thankful and appreciative about even the little things in life. People have those days when they're just in a grand funk, but overall they are thankful. A thankful attitude prepares the heart and mind to receive the energy and inspiration to flip the switch.

8. **Family relationships.** Family relationships can be tipping points moving us toward a positive flip of the switch, or they can be tripping points moving us into all kinds of difficulties and despair.

I've always appreciated the supportive nature of my family in my youth, and I deeply appreciate the support I receive from my family now. But some family relationships can be difficult and stressful, creating an atmosphere of distrust and bitterness. If you are in that kind of family situation, you must deal with it and learn to emotionally disengage from the drama. There are others who come to a new realization of how important their families are to them. Consider the story of another friend of mine.

■ ■ ■

Andrew Yang's Story

Not everyone's story of flipping the switch toward achievement and meaningfulness follows the same path. Everyone has a story about his or her life's journey and its crossroads—crossroads that helped define the future. Andrew Yang is an example of someone who has had his share of tipping points and used them in very positive ways.

Andrew Yang is Director of Golf, the Future's Course, at the 500 Club Golf Course in Scottsdale, Arizona. He is a PGA-approved professional golfer and trainer. I met Andrew at a golf course, was impressed with him, and employed him to give me golf lessons. He is not only an excellent golfer but a gifted instructor. The two don't always go hand in hand.

Andrew's instruction style is to build on students' abilities, not tear them down. In my case, he needed a construction crew! One of my favorite Andrew-isms is, "That was a very good miss!" At first, I thought he was kidding, but he was serious. His meaning is that I got the ball off the tee, and there is room for improvement. With me, there is a lot of room!

Of Chinese ancestry, Andrew's father is from Macau and his mother is from Hong Kong. His parents met in their late twenties in Arizona. Therefore, Arizona is the only home Andrew has ever known. Andrew is young but possesses composure beyond his age. He has a wife named Carisa, who is Italian.

Observing Andrew, one would never guess that his life held challenges. He is a polished person with impeccable manners; he is handsome, a talented athlete, exudes quiet confidence, and is sincerely interested in his students. He played golf in high school and, outside of work, engages his brother and father in the sport. His first assistant pro position was also at the same country club where he met his wife. Their first date was a wedding. She caught the bouquet and he caught the garter. That started a serious relationship.

After high school, Andrew felt pressure to select a college. He was tempted to enter military service, but his parents advised him to find an alternative. He had wanted to make his own decision, but looking back, he understands that it was good advice. Andrew became aware of a new program at Arizona State University: professional golf management studies (PGM). With the summer free, he decided to investigate the program. That, he contends, was one of the switch-flipping crossroads of his life. He didn't realize at the time of enrollment that his decision would place him in a cherished profession.

"It was a convenient opportunity," he explains. "It was just there at the time, and I took it." The PGM studies came under the auspices of the agribusiness department. He enrolled and received a bachelor of arts in agribusiness. It made sense that if golfers were to manage golf courses, the agribusiness degree would be valuable.

Though tempted at times to change majors, he stuck with the program in large part because he wanted to prove to himself that he could complete something that *he had actually chosen to do*. He had to live away from his parents and be on his own. Being away from his close-knit family, he had to make his own decisions and deal with the consequences.

Earlier I stated that Andrew's appearance would not indicate that he has had many challenges. It was at this point in his life that he encountered challenges in the form of drugs and alcohol. Andrew relates that those were tough times brought about by his decisions—decisions that prolonged finishing his degree.

"I had to make a lot of bad decisions before I realized what good choices are," he tells me with a sense of a man who has been to the brink of his downfall and stepped back from the edge. *That* is truly flipping the switch.

One of Andrew's traits that comes across loudly and clearly is that he is a profoundly thankful person. Andrew explains how hard his mom worked at the post office and his dad at his printing business to make college possible for him. He was the first in his family to graduate from college.

His thankfulness gave him the drive to finish college and be successful. During his challenging days of making bad decisions, he realized there was a "struggle between how I was raised and how I was living—and the two didn't align." Andrew went on to fulfill the requirements for the degree and for his PGA certification.

Through a family friend, Andrew accepted a job working at a resort. Having secured the position of first assistant golf pro, he also accepted more responsibility and stress. Again, a huge factor in getting him through it all was realizing what his parents had been through.

"If they could do it, so could I. It was a drive to succeed and prove myself. Career doesn't define me. I do it because I like it. When I leave it, I get into my family life and the next stages of my life." Balance is very important to him. "Career helps provide the other aspects, but family is the most important. I surround myself with those who think the same."

Ultimately, his position at the resort was eliminated as a cost-cutting measure. "It was out of my control, but it was necessary for my development." All the stress and challenges helped him learn more about life, career, and the value of hard work. Having Carisa in his life has been a huge benefit.

Finally, a giant factor in Andrew's ability to continually flip the switch is his faith. It is important to him.

"I haven't learned all my lessons yet. My parents instilled an appreciation of faith in my life. It is my belief. It helps me realize it's all in the plan. A calmness that comes from knowing a higher power. A lot of things happen that I don't need to understand and figure out. It helps me see lots of things in the rearview mirror that belong there."

Andrew's life could have taken wrong turns at a lot of points. And as he admits, there were some turns he took that were dead ends. The significant thinking he employed is that *he realized they were dead ends* and he put them where they belonged—in the rearview mirror of his life. Those teachable moments in his life were there because of his choices. To his credit, and to anyone's credit for that matter, is the fact that Andrew was teachable. A teachable moment cannot happen without the willingness to be taught. Andrew seized those moments, those "very good misses," learned something from them, flipped the switch, and set new directions in his life.

■ ■ ■

There are a multitude of events in life that can be either tripping points or flipping points, depending on how they are approached, such as

- a career or job change or loss;
- the loss of a loved one;
- divorce;
- a health and life threat;
- a financial loss;
- a financial gain (no, these are not always positive!);
- the birth of a child;
- marriage;
- a new home;
- a foreclosure; or
- religious issues.

In flipping the switch toward a more rewarding future and a healthier view of one's history, there are tipping points that may suddenly move an individual toward the flip of the switch.

Earlier, I introduced the enormous role that a perspective transformation often plays in flipping the switch. Tipping points are very similar with one important difference. A perspective transformation that brings about change is almost always an internal occurrence. Something mentally and emotionally moves inside the individual to bring a sudden awareness that the direction in which he or she is moving (or not moving) is totally wrong.

A tipping point can be an accumulation of events that gradually nudges the individual toward a different course of action, gives new insight about one's current state of affairs, or even coerces a person into moving forward. The accumulation of events puts a new spin on the seemingly comfortable state of homeostasis, whether it really is comfortable or not. What is perceived as a comfortable state of equilibrium may not be that at all after examining all the factors. Samuel Hoffenstein spoke tongue in cheek when he wrote the declaration, "Come weal, come woe, my status is quo." In reality, the status quo may be just an anesthetizing agent until you hit bottom!

In considering tripping and tipping points, Zachary Kurtz is one of those persons whose appreciation for his family was renovated after some difficult life experiences. His newfound sense of appreciation became a factor that tipped his consciousness toward a very positive life view.

■■■

Zachary Kurtz's Story

My wife and I met Zachary at Pastini Pastaria in Portland, Oregon. He was an excellent, attentive, efficient waiter for us. During a brief conversation with him, we discovered that he had some definite ideas about how life should be lived. Zachary mentioned that, to him, organic was about more than food. That statement, his positive and confident demeanor, along with details about his life, prompted me to ask if he would meet with me for a longer conversation. To my delight, he replied that he would love to. We met at a grocery store that was also a coffee bar and restaurant—a wonderful place to have a conversation. We spent nearly three hours talking nonstop.

This interesting twenty-three-year-old had a lot of wisdom for his age. Zachary was another example of someone who had tasted many of the flavors of life and had learned to discriminate between them. Some he found to be good and embraced them. Others he found distasteful and wisely rejected them. It was all a part of flipping the switch for his life.

Zachary was born and reared in Virginia Beach, Virginia, along with his two siblings. His father was a navy mechanic in San Diego, California, in the late eighties. From there, his family moved to Kansas with the promise of an even better job for his dad. However, soon after they moved, his dad lost that job through no fault of his own. Next came a move to West Virginia. Zachary told me that his dad was one of those people who would work his heart out to provide for his family.

The man regularly worked two jobs and sometimes had as many as four jobs at once. He worked long hours on the road as a trucker, delivering Volvo tractors for tractor-trailer outfitters. He wasn't home much. He missed most of the events of Zachary's teenage years—ball games, family vacations, and more.

Zachary resented his dad for being gone and not attending his games and other events. He was conspicuous by his absence. It's hard to explain to a kid that a parent is away from home because he or she has to make that sacrifice for the financial stability of the family. The explanations don't always reach the emotional level of a child. Back then, Zachary had to find his own rides to his ball games, stay even-keeled, become self-sufficient, learn to cook, and push himself to communicate his needs to other adults.

At about age fourteen, Zachary experienced a transition in his life. Since he was used to being with his sisters and his mom, he began to feel bitter about times when his dad was home. In his early teens, he was becoming his own person, perhaps beyond his years. Zachary rebelled against his dad's authority. They clashed. High school went downhill because of another move, resulting in the loss of his friends and his cherished sports activities. He found it difficult transitioning into the new school. Athletics had always been his main outlet—no movies, shopping, or similar activities.

Zachary's grades dropped. He began hanging out with the wrong crowd. Eventually, he dropped out of high school as a junior at age sixteen. Elemental to his future, he discovered a mariner school in Virginia and enrolled. He attended the Seafarers International Union (SIU) school full time. Having inherited his dad's determined spirit, he put his mind and body to the effort and did well. Through SIU, he completed his high school program and also traveled abroad.

Tripping points could have easily come for Zachary at this stage. He could have held onto his resentment toward his dad and nurtured it. He could have accepted less from himself mentally and emotionally as an adult and blamed it on the circumstances of his rearing. But there came a point in his life when Zachary "became *thankful* to his dad for what he had been willing to do for his family." Those very things that he saw as difficult and uncomfortable in his adolescence, such as having to become self-sufficient, he recognized as valuable gifts for his adult years.

Not everyone sees life that way. Some people see the difficulties and nothing beyond them. For Zachary, it became a choice to do some significant thinking about his life. Further, he flipped the switch from thinking what could and would diminish him, to thinking what would give him thankfulness and determination to succeed.

Zachary relates that the flipping of his switch had been due to what he put into himself—both into his mind and into his body. He credits Deepak Chopra's *The Book of Secrets* with helping him transform both his attitude and his spiritual nature. To Zachary, it's all about asking the right questions about anything one encounters, especially about oneself.

Zachary wisely contends that quality of life can be directly related to knowing how to ask questions. "Stop and ask, 'Is this what I believe, or what someone else told me to believe?' Explore those uncomfortable, vulnerable times and your life and mind will expand—spiritually, relationally, politically, and mentally."

Through his difficulties, Zachary learned some things that helped him flip. *He learned to wake up.* Part of that waking up was also making up. That is, setting things straight with his dad and showing appreciation. That in itself is such a health-promoting event. He also learned that negative interactions could either drive one to isolation or to communion with others. Lastly, he learned to become self-directed in a big way, referencing his completing high school through the Seafarers International Union.

As for the future, Zachary is optimistic that he will be able to play a positive role in making the American food culture one that promotes health. In fact, he is already doing that through his work with other groups that promote healthy lifestyles and by leading workshops on nutrition. Zachary believes that an important question for health is, "What is a better way to eat?"

His passions are organic food and organic living. Zachary wants to see American society come to the point where healthy options for food are not only on as many street corners as fast food, but that they become as popular as fast-food choices. He continues to look for ways to become a part of that transition in society. Zachary also does one-on-one nutritional lifestyle counseling and finds that very rewarding. It is interesting that Zachary is very passionate about his mission, but he is not offensive in his sharing of it with others. Through his calm, almost Zen-like personality, he attracts people to his cause.

Making It Personal

1. **Review the examples of tripping points and tipping points in chapter twelve.**
2. **Do any of the examples resonate with you?** If so, which ones?
3. **Take some time to let your mind process the question.** Why does this example resonate with me? Is it because I need to work on that part of my attitude or outlook?

CHAPTER 13
Step into Your Future

Krystol Stemm's Story

Krystol flipped a huge switch in her life a few years ago. She flipped a switch that many in American society wish they could accomplish. She lost *sixty pounds in six months and has kept it off.* To look at this trim, petite, but athletically built woman, one would never guess that she was once obese.

In fact, Krystol flipped a lot of switches in a relatively short period of time. Some personalities flip life-direction switches over a period of time. Others find the crush of life situations so immediate that a singular flip toward a different direction is not sufficient. They find a virtual storm of switch flipping is necessary.

Interestingly, Krystol related her successful weight loss story to me toward the end of my interview with her. It is clear that she does not want her former obesity to define her now any more than she wanted it to define her then.

Krystol comes from what she terms a "multi-dysfunctional family." She was born in Ventura, California, and has an older sister and two half siblings. Her mother has been remarried for thirty-four years, and her father for twenty-three years. She was reared in a moderate lifestyle. Early in her life, her father moved away after the divorce. Her grandparents became very influential in her life from about age six. Her grandparents were a stabilizing force in her life at a time when her alcoholic stepfather was emotionally abusing her mother, Krystol, and her siblings. Her stepfather has now been sober for over ten years.

In spite of all the instability, Krystol was outgoing in high school. She reveals that she was very disappointed that her parents did not attend more of her events. Every child wants validation, but Krystol didn't receive it. She and her mom had difficulty communicating effectively. Partially to escape her mom and partially to escape her stepfather, Krystol moved in with her dad and two stepsiblings for two years. She excelled in volleyball, which was a lifeline for her. Yet she explains, "I still made some poor decisions due to lack of support and guidance, and having to become an adult early in life."

One day, Krystol came home from school to discover that her stepmother had cleaned out the house, removing all of her dad's belongings. It seemed her stepmother had discovered her dad's lack of commitment to the marriage. It had been slipping for years.

After high school, Krystol continued to play volleyball, attending college in San Diego and playing for the college team. It was on this that she could focus and excel, instead of focusing on her family. Her grandmothers helped with her college expenses. Krystol demonstrates that she has a grateful attitude by expressing her appreciation to those grandmothers for their help at that crucial time in her life, and at other crucial times.

It was in college that Krystol met a US Air Force man. She gives him credit for helping her clearly see the nature of her family and, more importantly, the strained relationship with her older sibling that caused some problems with family members. She moved in with the man and later followed him to Idaho. She acknowledges that she made some unwise decisions. He later became involved in another relationship, they broke up, and she moved back to California and in with her dad. Her boyfriend called to reconcile, but Krystol flipped a switch at that point and dumped him.

Soon came another heavy time in Krystol's life. At age twenty-one, she acquired a DUI. She lost her driver's license and consequently her job, and she had to drop out of college. For the first time in over a decade, she lost her independence.

Eventually, Krystol flipped the switch from letting the history of high-maintenance relationships with her family hold her back in life toward a more rewarding, fulfilling, and satisfying life. Instead of focusing on the negative, Krystol began to realize what assets she had at her disposal and began using those to help her move onward and upward! She realized that though she had not received a sense of groundedness from her parents, she had gotten a model for a solid life from other families and from her grandparents.

Cherri, whom she calls her "BFF," and Cherri's parents were very stabilizing forces for Krystol.

She eventually met and married the love of her life. During their fifteen years of marriage so far, they have produced two wonderful sons. She and her husband are dedicated to rearing the children in a functional, loving family. Krystol went on to become a regional manager for Nordstrom department stores and has received awards for outstanding performance. She later resigned that position to focus on her family, due to her youngest son being diagnosed with autism at age four. Krystol says she has learned a tremendous amount of patience through her son's challenges. As he has aged, she has found more time to return to work and school.

As you read Krystol's life story, you surely noticed that she didn't flip the switch from inertia to forward movement just once. She had to do it several times as situations arose to confront her. Each time her life became richer—not necessarily easier, but richer. She created her own sense of groundedness through her husband and children, involvement in academics, a career, and returning to the mainstream of social involvement. Krystol is very proud that she was given the customer service all-star award at work.

Krystol has had many flipping points in her life. "The air force man thing," as she calls it, showed her what she would and would not tolerate from men. It also told her what she would and would not tolerate from family members. Another point was confronting the challenges and tremendous rewards of rearing a child with autism.

Then, when Krystol's weight reached two hundred pounds due to the stress in her life, she made what she calls "a huge life change." She decided to focus on herself and get healthy for her own sake, but also for the sake of her children. That's when she lost sixty pounds, and five years later, she has kept it off. The flip here was a perspective transformation on how she saw herself in relation to her health. She dropped the relationships that did not reward her, and in so doing, she dropped a lot of stress to lose the weight.

"I never thought I could do anything. I lived for recognition and affirmation. Whenever I get compliments or recognition, I get validation," Krystol says about herself. She learned that she could do much indeed. The switch that flipped for her was creating a stable, loving marriage and family, along with flourishing work accomplishments.

Krystol's biggest hope is that "my kids will not have the family relationships that I have had." She wants her children to have a stable, wholesome family with relationships that mirror those values. She also wants them to have good decision-making processes. "We're here to shape these kids to become good adults."

Krystol has done some great switch flipping. She moved from periods in her life when she was allowing herself to be acted upon, to the point of realizing she could move beyond reactive thinking to becoming a self-directed person. She describes it well: "I now realize that life's journey is an evolution."

■ ■ ■

It is my hope that by now you have been mentally moved

- *from* "I can't" *to* "I can." You may not have started out completely in the "I can't" state. You may have been at "if I can't" or even "if I can." In any case, I truly hope you are in the "I can" state of being;
- *from* reactive thinking *to* reflective thinking; and
- *from* a lack of passion and vision for your life *to* a sense of hope and direction for your future.

So now do it! Step into your future. Here are five important directions for how to take those steps.

1. Keep close at hand the notes you made while you read this book. You did do the exercises, right? Review those from time to time to help keep you focused and motivated.
2. I reemphasize the need for a life coach, mentor, or other person who will keep you accountable as you step into your future. I keep in regular contact with some of the people whom I have coached and mentored to check on their progress, to offer encouragement, to challenge, and to congratulate them on making progress. I have found that most people need some or all of that, especially those who are in life situations (job, family, relationships, etc.) that can eat up their initiative, money, and time. It's hard to step away from the anesthesia of complacency. But two things help: having a place to step toward and the determination to do so.

3. As you step into your future, don't take everything with you. As a perhaps oversimplified example, imagine yourself packing for a long trip. Since I dislike packing, I tend to take a bit more in my suitcase than I really need. That's one of the positive things about the weight limit on airplanes! It forces me to be more careful about what I throw in that suitcase.

   As you think about packing for a trip, you may ask, "If I take this item, will I really use it?" or "Do I really need so many changes of clothes?" or "Do I want to haul all this stuff around with me?" Pulling and lifting a lot of dead weight is a good way to promote reevaluation of what to pack for a trip.

   Similarly, as you step into your future, consider what you may want to leave behind. In a more positive way of saying it, consider what you may want to take with you. Both considerations are important. You should leave behind

- *negativism about yourself, others, and the world.* That is a lot to do! And you will have to work at it. But here's why I want you to do all three. Because *all three are connected.* It is difficult, if not downright impossible, to be positive about yourself if you are negative about the world around you and your relationships. And besides, it's very unattractive! I'm sure you can recall being with someone who was so self-deprecating that you started looking around for an exit.

A *little* self-deprecation can be charming. It may let others know that you don't take yourself too seriously. But it may also come across as just pathetic! It can be uncomfortable being with someone who has a negative world view and who is suspicious and distrustful of people. Where's that exit? So make a decided effort to leave those attitudes behind. Again, as mentioned in an earlier section, it is better to go *to* something than to simply go *from* something. In this case, you are flipping the switch toward a more balanced, healthy view of yourself, others, and the world.

- *habits that keep you repeatedly and eternally rolling the stone up the hill.* I always feel a little sorry for Wile E. Coyote. No matter how he tries, he never seems to be able to catch the Road Runner who seems to be blissfully unaware that he's even being pursued! Wile E. is the personification of one definition of insanity: doing the same thing over and over and expecting a different result. Why doesn't Wile E. change his strategies? Why doesn't he seek different prey? Why doesn't he realize that his skill set doesn't fit with pursuing an inappropriate goal?

There are two things you can do that will require some bravery on your part. One, list some of the habits of which you are aware that hinder you. Remember the cutting and growing edges discussed earlier? Second, use the person you choose to hold you accountable to also hold you accountable for leaving behind bad habits.

For example, maybe you have the habit of overtalking in a conversation or overexpressing your thoughts on any subject that is brought up. Try slowing yourself down in conversations and thinking more about what you are preparing to say. The result may be that when you do speak, others will truly hear what you have to say and respond more positively.

You should take with you

- *the realization that you have flipped the switch in your life.* The realization that you have made the determination to change those aspects of your life should give you a feeling of peace and progress. Take those feelings with you and refer to them often. The fact that you get it, that you understand what flipping the switch is all about, can help stabilize your emotional foundation and help you step into your future.
- *a sense of peace.* For me, just knowing that I am working toward a solution and stepping into my future gives me a sense of peace. It doesn't replace the hard work of keeping the switch flipped and moving forward, but actions that replace inertia and angst add great fuel to the flipping efforts.
- *an action plan.* Suppose someone is robbing your house. Imagine yourself holding the door open

for him as he repeatedly carries items out and returns for more. You just stand there and allow him to do it! Of course, you would never do that unless you were being forced to comply. What you *would* do is seek safety for yourself and your family, call the police, and take other appropriate measures to *stop the loss and rectify the situation!* You would immediately come up with a plan because of the sense of urgency that has intruded into your life.

Similarly, along with that sense of peace referred to earlier, there should be a sense of urgency about the issues that you have identified in your life. Out of that sense of urgency, there must be a plan of action. There is a difference between urgency and panic or desperation. The biggest difference for switch flippers is that urgency may stimulate action, yet give room enough to plan in a solid and thoughtful way. Panic may stimulate a plan, but it is very prone to mistakes and inappropriate, dangerous, and ineffective results.

- *a sense of humor.* Most people who know me know that I love humor. It has been a real and present help in times of trouble. Life without humor would be dull and colorless. So along the route of achieving the ends that you have defined, make sure one of the means to those ends is an appreciation for the humor in almost any situation.

    Not all humor is the laughing kind. Some humor recognizes the absurdity in certain undertakings.

Another kind of humor may give the individual an awareness of his or her own vulnerability. That is, it may cause you or someone else to realize that the whole world does not rest on your shoulders. And certainly, healthy humor does not make fun of nor demean anyone, or cause anyone to think less of himself than you would want to think of yourself.

- *a healthy work ethic.* A healthy work ethic is one that is *integrated into the rest of your life.* Often people mistakenly define their work ethic in terms of how many hours per week they give to the job. Or it is defined as how hard they drive themselves in their career. What they don't realize is that a healthy work ethic is not defined so much by the *intensity* of their efforts as it is by the *integrity* of those efforts.

A work ethic that has integrity is simply one that is *integrated into a balanced lifestyle.* A work ethic that has integrity will make sure that the intensity of effort does not overwhelm the other elements of life. If you are using an accelerated approach to your job or career while stealing quality time and attention from other elements of your life, then it is not a healthy work ethic. It is not what I call a purposefully selected life ethic.

A purposefully selected lifestyle ethic chooses the elements of that lifestyle rather than letting elements choose it. When I was studying for my oral comprehensive exams at Indiana University and writing my dissertation, there were times when I felt overwhelmed by a full-time job, family, civic obligations, aging parents, youth and adult mentorship, and on and on. Finally, it dawned on me that I was too driven in some areas of my life. I realized that I was unintentionally shortchanging my wife, my children, and myself. I made changes. I did not give up on my doctoral work, but I did scale it back. For example, I did more studying and writing after our family time in the evenings. Often, that meant not beginning the university work until late at night.

Therefore, as you step into your future, make sure you choose decisively a work ethic that is integrated into the rest of your life and the lives of those around you.

4. From time to time, review the significant thinking principles. Remember that

- **any thinking that does not move you forward diminishes you;**
- **as thinking begins to open up, so do possibilities;**
- **moonlight is better than no light; and**
- **going *toward* something is better than going *from* something.**

Make it a habit to think in those terms. Think in terms that move you forward. Open up your mind, and open up your personal possibilities. Go with what light you have, rather than cursing the darkness. Determine to go *toward* your fulfillment rather than running *away* from your problems.

5. This is urgent. Frame it. *If you trip and fall—and you will—***get back up!** Unless you are superhuman, there will be times when you stumble and fall as you step into your future. There are going to be times when you feel discouraged. There are going to be times when you think you are a failure. There are going to be times when the ball is on your two-yard line and they've been scoring on you all day. There will be times when you want to say, "I've had it! I quit! It's just easier to stay in my complacency and inertia. I'll go back to 'I can't' and live there. I can't do this!"

At those times, get back in touch with your life coach. Get back in touch with your accountability and support person. Most importantly, get back in touch with *yourself.* Ask yourself, what will give you the most fulfillment—quitting or achieving? Most times of discouragement and pain encountered after the flip of the switch can be alleviated by reviewing your reasons *for* flipping the switch in the first place. It was because you were dissatisfied and unfulfilled with your life or some aspect of it.

A word about testing. I would be remiss if I did not mention the benefits of personality and aptitude testing. The purpose of which, is to help you better understand your potential inclinations toward certain careers or interests.

Testing may also reveal aspects of your personality that contribute to your perceptions and actions. Below are only two examples.

Using yes and no answers, the Minnesota Multiphasic Personality Inventory (MMPI) is a tool used by trained professionals in assessing an individual's personality traits. Upon entering the doctoral program at Indiana University, I was required to take the MMPI. I found that it was very good at pinpointing certain aspects of my personality without making any value judgments about those traits. For example, the test revealed that I was apt to take on multiple tasks and then feel overwhelmed. Fitting with that finding, it also pointed out that I carried a lot of stress that, in turn, contributed to my lack of a sense of security. Being aware of those traits became a valuable tool in helping me flip the switch toward better coping skills.

The Strong-Campbell Interest Inventory (SII) Indicator is another very useful tool. Unlike the MMPI, the SII helps identify the individual's interests for career development or for one's own personal development. I like this test because, coupled with the MMPI, you will gain a sense of your personality traits and a starting point in assessing career interests and aptitudes that could be appropriate for you. Again, only you can make the determination whether the test results are valid for your life.

Another time-proven tool is the Meyers-Briggs Type Indicator (MBTI). The Meyers and Briggs Foundation website gives a succinct definition of the MBTI:

The purpose of the Myers-Briggs Type Indicator® (MBTI®) personality inventory is to make the theory of psychological types described by C. G. Jung understandable and useful in people's lives. The essence of the theory is that much seemingly random variation in behavior is actually quite orderly and consistent, being due to basic differences in the way individuals prefer to use their perception and judgment.

I have taken the MBTI many times. The thing I like about it most is its ability to indicate types of behavior that are not concrete, but ones that may change over time or in various situations.

For example, one possible combination of indicators may cluster to reveal that an individual is an ENTJ personality. Oversimplified, it means that in most situations, an ENTJ personality may get energy by focusing on extroversion rather than introversion, may take in information by intuition rather than using the five senses, may make decisions based on thinking it through rather than feeling what is right, or may look at the world around him or her with a predominantly logical view rather than a empathetic one.

Another aspect I like about the MBTI is that it gives guidelines about what personality types tend to work well together. That cross-relational information can be extremely useful in the workplace, in committee or task force compositions, in premarital and marriage counseling, and in conflict management, to name only a few.

I am not an expert on personality, aptitude, or career testing. However, I can testify to the benefits of testing for my career and relationships in general. I urge you to contact a high school or college near you to learn which tests you should take for your particular purposes. Another source of information on testing may be your employer's human resources department. Using this source may reward you with continuing education credits. Additionally, your employer may subsidize the cost of the testing.

I trust that, as you read this book, you underlined, dog-eared, highlighted, or by some other method marked areas that caught your attention. Perhaps those areas made you think in a different way about yourself. Go back and reread the words that made you think. Thumb through them, and refresh the feelings of purpose that were generated in your heart and mind when you first read them.

Finally, as you step into your future, please know that my thoughts and prayers are with you as you flip the switch in your life. I would very much like to know of your efforts and achievements. You may contact me through the publisher or through my e-mail: fliptheswitch0245@gmail.com.

About
Dr. Wm. Wayne Brown

The author has a passion for assisting individuals toward good decision-making by learning how to use Significant Thinking Principles. Through a long history of mentoring, Dr. Brown assists individuals toward the realization that *how* they think is as important as *what* they think. He contends "*Any thinking that does not move you forward diminishes you*" (p. 16). His career as a public speaker, teacher, fundraiser, and minister has been guided by that concept. Throughout his career, Dr. Brown has been passionate about coaching individuals toward greater achievement and fulfillment. He serves as a mentor and life coach through his organization, Life Designs Consulting.

Dr. Brown was born and raised in Marion, Kentucky. He graduated from Georgetown College (BA), Georgetown,

Kentucky, the Southern Theological Seminary (MDiv), Louisville, Kentucky, and from the Indiana University School of Education (EdD), Bloomington, Indiana. His doctoral studies focused on higher education administration and adult learning. His dissertation is an analysis of factors contributing to the nonparticipation of adults in learning opportunities. An earlier publication, "Willie Loman Has a Crisis of Limits," was published in *Lifelong Learning: The Adult Years*. He has served on numerous religious and educational committees, boards of directors across the country, and as a trustee for two colleges.

He served as executive director of an ecclesiastical nonprofit judicatory for fourteen years and as a pastor for fifteen years. He served as adjunct professor of adult and community development at Ball State University's Graduate School of Education, Muncie, Indiana, and the MBA program at Indiana Wesleyan University, Marion, Indiana. He has been guest speaker at various venues and teaching/learning formats. Additionally, he chaired the Research Committee for the Indiana Governor's Taskforce on Literacy.

Dr. Brown is married to C. Yvonne Brown, who authored a portion of the book series, *Chocolate for a Woman's Spirit*. The Browns live in Beaverton, Oregon. He is available for private and group consultation, as well as for speaking engagements. Contacts may be made through this email address: fliptheswitch0245@gmail.com

Made in United States
Troutdale, OR
12/13/2024